Mama said...
It's the small victories that count!

3ᴿᴰ EDITION

Bonnie J. Edwards, M.A.Ed., Author
Professional Development & Training
A resource and guidebook for educators, parents, and students

MAMA SAID…IT'S THE SMALL VICTORIES THAT COUNT!
Copyright © 2018 **Bonnie J. Edwards**

All rights reserved. No part of this book may be used or reproduced by any means, graphic, electronic, or mechanical, including photocopying, recording, taping or by information storage and retrieval system without the written permission of the author except in the case of brief quotations embodied in critical articles and reviews.

Stratton Press, LLC
1603 Capitol Ave, Suite 310,
Cheyenne, WY 82001
www.stratton-press.com
1-888-323-7009

Because of the dynamic nature of the Internet, any web addresses or links contained in this book may have changed since publication and may no longer be valid. The views expressed in the work are solely those of the author and do not necessarily reflect the views of the publisher, and the publisher hereby disclaims any responsibility for them.

ISBN (Paperback): 978-1-947355-63-7
ISBN (Hardback): 978-1-64345-358-3
ISBN (Ebook): 978-1-64345-063-6

Printed in the United States of America

Contents

Acknowledgements 7
Preface 9
Foreword 15
Chapter 1: Mama's presence 21
Chapter 2: A time for learning 29
Chapter 3: Mama checks in 34
Chapter 4: A problem is solved 39
Chapter 5: Bonita's transformation 44
Chapter 6: A sense of Pride 51
Communication/Companion 57
    Introduction 58
    Pearls of Wisdom 62
    DISCUSSION…Self-reflective Models for
        Extended Teaching and Lifelong Learning 76
    "Making The Case For Joyce Epstein's
        Six Types of Family Involvement" 90
    The Keeper of the Fire 97
    The Case For Character Education Integration into a K-12
        School Curriculum 117
Memory Lane 124
Appendices 135
References 139
Resources 141
Contact Us 145

In Loving Memory of

*my loving, compassionate, and
Christian mother who taught me how to be
a decent, God fearing and compassionate
individual. To someone who also taught me how
to stick to my dreams and to never be afraid
to dedicate my life to service. I will forever
cherish my mother, her wisdom, her incredible
strength as a woman and her everlasting
inspiration. This book is for you Mama.*

Acknowledgements

To my loving and honorable father who made this book a dream come true. Daddy, you are one of a kind. You fill my heart with the great wonders of the world. You have taught me how to walk, talk, and behave like a lady. I am a stronger women and person because you love me unconditionally. I feel truly blessed to have you as my father.

To Cary, my loving, devoted husband and biggest fan who kept me grounded throughout this entire process. Editors cannot compare to you. With your timely wisdom and especially creative touches, this story came to life! No one could have sprinkled those special moments like you have for me. You are my gift from God. I can't thank you enough. Mama would say, "Well done."

To Danny, our son. You encouraged me in ways that sons could by offering words of inspiration and loving thoughts about what it is like for youngsters to grow up today. Thank you for challenging me to think like the youth of today. I had great conversations with you as I reflected on my own childhood memories. I am proud of you.

To Lisa and Mildred, our daughters, mama said those who bring expressions of sunshine into a room help others feel the warmth of their smiles too. I am proud to see the beautiful ladies you have become.

To my Pastor, Rev. B.J. Gaston, (Uncle Bennie) who has not only been part of my life but in my life. How do I thank someone who has been so special to me in all aspects of my life? You always said, "Bonnie, I saw you before you were born." Your image of me has stuck with me all of my life. Thank you for being my Pastor all of my life, and I pray for your continued spiritual guidance as I continue to work and fulfill God's will.

To my sisters and brothers, my hope is that other families feel a sense of appreciation for close family ties and feel inspired by their own personal stories. This story is a reflection of all of our childhood experiences. My love and respect for all of you is stellar and grounded in faith. Above all, we had the extra bonus to feature one of our beautiful and adorable nieces, Dorthel who gave this story a timeless and visual representation. What more could a new author ask for. I will always love and appreciate all of you because we all are reflections of our loving mother.

Linda, a historian in your own right, not to mention the love and strength you continue to show us as our big sister. Mama always said, "family first." You continue to instill in us the importance of family ties. I love you Linda!

To my dear friend Joan. You continue to be a faithful friend. Thank you for your continued friendship and inspiration.

It's been said that sometimes a child's positive school experience has little to do with what they learn but how the teacher made them feel. As my elementary school teacher Mrs. McWilliams, you were all that and more to me.

PREFACE

Reflection and the Journey
Bonnie J. Edwards, M.A.Ed

My personal and professional goals are diverse. I am a lifelong learner. My pursuit to continue learning in a higher education environment is a natural extension of who I am as an individual and practitioner. The Teacher Leadership specialization is designed for educators who want to continue teaching while assuming influential roles in their school and community. The piece that seals it for me is the specialization's focus on "Educator as Leader." For several years, I have engaged myself in the type of changes that empowers teachers. The major goal is always improving student learning and engaging parents.

Sixteen years ago, shortly before 9/11, my mother, friend, my heart and confidant died from heart and lung complications at West Allis Memorial Hospital. I was devastated. I felt as though my life was sucked right out of me. My mother's passing came at a time when I was writing a column for the Wisconsin Woman Magazine Inc. The next issue would be written about Mother's Day. One of the last conversations I had with my mother was the possibility of becoming a teacher. Honestly, I didn't see it in my future but apparently my mother did. At that time I remembered what my mother said about me as an individual and what she said stuck with me. My mother reminded me about the joy I got out of helping others. She also reminded me of how much I enjoyed being around people and my ability to work with children and adults.

I listened to my mother and pursued a second career in education. I'm pleased to share what I learned and discovered during my pursuit. One important aspect of teaching and learning is practicing effective communication. The first and second editions of Mama Said...It's the Small Victories That Count provided the basis for forward-thinking and the importance of communicating in a school community. I think effective communication is lacking in our schools. I've come to this realization because I have seen that many students feel they are not being listened to by their teachers. In addition, some parents are feeling overwhelmed just with meeting the day-to-day needs of their children. Without question, a host of teachers are beginning to feel more and more isolated from their colleagues and classrooms are becoming more difficult to manage. I think my son said it well, "Have teachers forgotten what it's like to be kids?" His point deserved attention.

Let us examine these questions: Should the education community work harder to reach out to students and their families? Are we asking a little too much from our teachers given that they also have homes to manage, prepare dinner for their families, shopping, engage in their children's educational affairs? Maybe, but perhaps the educational community could dig a little deeper in building stronger and deeper relationships with their students and families. Is it unrealistic for us to expect teachers to apply some of the communication strategies they may use with their own children to work with their classroom students? I think this idea is worth exploring. These beliefs I have are products of my personal and professional experiences. My values are integral of what I believe about teaching and learning and the most effective ways to achieve both. By specializing in middle school teaching, professional development, administrative leadership, and instructional design, these entities provides a needed pathway to identify, question, test, evaluate, and apply theories that speaks to my educational beliefs and philosophy. This platform as a writer allows me to do that. As a messenger of viable information, I can help, support, and advance teachers as leaders in their profession and within their school communities. This can be accomplished through public discourse, community outreach, teacher mentorships, student participation, parental engagement, effective administrative leadership, and educational policy.

My previous undergraduate and graduate academic experience has raised my passion for communication, the understanding of attitudes and the behavior it provides. I've dedicated my life to educating children and adults. This is indicative of my commitment to teaching in an urban educational environment for the past fourteen years. My work as an edu-

cator extends outside the classroom to professional development. This 3rd Edition allows me to extend those and new ideas to continue the dialog.

Additionally, my experience in traveling abroad has played a key role in my choice of study. An independent study enabled me to visit Israel in 1997 as part of a holy pilgrimage with the late Reggie White of the Green Bay Packers. This was an experience of a lifetime and literally changed my life and personal mission to pursue an educational career. That experience along with other unique opportunities with traveling to Sacramento, CA, to serve on an advisory committee for the Wisconsin Department of Public Instruction for state testing were unimaginable accomplishments in my quest to become an effective teacher leader. As an engaged author, publisher, lecturer, speaker, wife, mother, daughter, my goal is to create a model for educators to use immediately in their classrooms and their school communities.

This 3rd Edition has provided the catalyst to share and use to inform others on the possibilities. The 2nd Edition established the foundation for starting the conversation using Mama said…(3) Pearls of Wisdom. This book used as a framework reinforces the principles taught at McPherson College-Milwaukee Campus in the Continuing Education program to educators; Interpersonal Communication: "Using Your Sphere of Influence." It is my belief that making connections with others for the purpose of building relationships is paramount for teacher leaders and administrators in all forms of school communities.

My husband reaffirms this idea by reminding me that "Using Your Sphere of Influence" is universal. He is right. We need to communicate to be effective in all walks in life. Oftentimes misunderstandings occur because individuals underestimate their ability to influence others toward positive change. I look forward to building on my knowledge as an effective communicator and educator using best practices as well as my own understanding and observations in promoting social change.

As an educator, I am constantly seeking avenues to conduct research related to student achievement and teacher engagement. More specifically, I am interested in pursuing ways for educators, through exploration and research to build better and stronger relationships with their students and families to improve student achievement. This 3rd Edition, Mama Said…It's the Small Victories That Count, with the Communication

Companion reiterates the basic premise and that is *Using Your Influence: Making Connections and Building Relationships with Others.*

This 3rd Edition hones in on examples and ideas that others may have experienced in their school communities. Some people will argue that communication is not the problem in our schools. However, others feel public education has not kept up with the demands of technology. Yes, technology has affected the way we live and communicate on a basic level. However, I believe the issues are greater and more human. Educators have an opportunity to learn about how communication theories can be used as strategies for understanding the human behavior and learning in educational settings. For instance, Maslow's Hierarchy of Needs can help teachers understand why a student lacks motivation to learn. What about Johari's Window and its theory on the importance of self-awareness? This means helping teachers understand the need to be open to the ideas of parents on how to reach their children. Last but not least, how often do teachers and parents forget to praise children when they are making good choices? Albert Bandura says it well when he reminds us that children need to know that adults care and believe in them and in turn they will believe in themselves. My hope is to contribute to the field of research by introducing new ways of thinking in academia. Ways I believe will move us in a direction that could benefit everyone, or least start the conversation. The 3rd Edition with the Communication Companion offers the 5 Ws of Communication. The simple guideline provides a description for each "W" represented in the book on how to best apply and implement the book's content when using the Communication Companion. This can be found in the later section of the book.

As my window of understanding continues to expand, I felt a jolt of energy to share new studies as well as practices which are illustrated in the 2nd and 3rd issues. I would encourage you to visit my website "Mama Said…It's the small victories that count" with The Communication Companion, 2nd Edition, on raising the awareness of family communication. You will discover this lighthearted story featuring an adolescent girl and her wise mother. The settings of the story are home, church, and a school community.

I have had the honor to work in the communication and educational fields with some of the most talented and finest professionals in the State of Wisconsin, Illinois, Texas, Colorado, and Georgia. Licensed educators are taught how to use their "Sphere of Influence" with their students, families, and colleagues utilizing interpersonal communication strategies. Characteristics may include effective listening, nonverbal communication skills, and relationship building. This course is also designed for educators to improve on their communication skills in a school community. Each time this course is presented, I'm inspired by the amazing educators (teachers, administrators) I meet that provides stellar insight and creative skills in bridging gaps that will improve communication among a school communities. It is that kind of electricity that gives me the energy to research and write about what works in schools and what does not.

This 3rd Edition with the Communication Companion gets to the core of human creativity and compassion. This course for educators as well as trainers was an approved three-credit graduate course by the Wisconsin Department of Public Instruction. Additionally, this course has been introduced in other professional venues including the Wisconsin Educational Association Council Teachers Conference, Milwaukee Teachers' Educational Association (MTEA) Community Partnerships, and in local schools. The major themes in all three editions are developed, delivered, and shared with individuals across the United States working in business, nursing, social work, counseling, business, and education.

Knowledge is power and sharing that information is even more powerful. Parents and educational leaders benefit from quality information and programs that will impact their communities in positive ways. I'm reminded of the benefits of reflecting on public broadcasting programs. These programs can be seen as catalysts for understanding educational policy, student behaviors, student performance, parent engagement, leadership, and teacher stewardship. It is my belief that when we pay attention to the pulse of our community, we begin to appreciate the obstacles and challenges others experience in their life. We witness others overcoming incredible odds—from complex layers of homelessness to the hills of hopefulness. Bringing solutions to issues, such as building relationships with parents to help their children become the best they can be, is what motivates me.

I love helping others. As I reflect on my life, it becomes more apparent to me that helping and serving others is living a purposeful life. We learn how to solve problems by listening, observing, and learning about other people's experiences and contributions.

My purpose as an educator and professional communicator is clearer today. My goals and dreams always revert back to my mother. This 3rd Edition reinforces many of her philosophies. My mother understood what barriers can get in the way of educating a student. We need to go back to the basics of teaching and learning. As educators and professionals, we should never underestimate our ability to influence children, students, or their parents. One of the best experiences I ever had was in my Graduate Program in the Department of Education at Alverno College, in Milwaukee, Wisconsin. Through that experience, I learned about the importance of listening to others, teamwork, problem-solving, critical thinking, having compassion, valuing others, and consensus building. I understood what it meant to be proactive and a problem-solver. This is indicative by the many professional projects I engaged in over my professional career. Also in this 3rd Edition with the Communication Companion, you will discover my understanding and support for Character Education in school communities. In summary, we must not give up. Our students and their families are counting on us. In the spirit of my mother, "It's the small victories that count." May her legacy continue to touch the spirit of families, students, parents, and educators.

Foreword

The sights and smells of our memories form who we are and what we initially value in life. Bonnie J. Edwards has captured the memories, the teachings, the warmth and the aromas of a childhood long gone, but lessons never forgotten. She weaves vignettes in a tapestry filled with joy, uncertainty, tears, and triumph through the lens of a young woman in search of herself and her identity. But unlike most writings of the decade, her search is steeped in a strong sense of family, love, and a village of support systems that work together to wrap their arms around her as she shapes and molds her values and vision for the future.

Food is a culture. Deals have been made and broken in rooms where food is prepared and shared over the ages. Mama's kitchen is her castle, the space where she dispenses wisdom, guidance and love in an atmosphere of culinary delights. You can feel her matriarchal power leap through the pages in an arc of overwhelming comfort and safety. She is the master teacher and master coach. She ensures that the setting for a sound family structure is maintained, while never missing a step in making each individual family member (yes - that includes you Daddy!) value the time she spends individually with them. The ability to set the tone and control the home environment makes her the quintessential heroine - strong, yet gentile - as her lessons emerge as a bright light throughout the theme of this book.

This is a must read for anyone who values family, understands the need to stay connected with family, and also harbors an occasional need to just close your eyes to see and smell the memories. You can see yourself in Mama's kitchen, or grab your own opportunity to translate her teachings to your family structure. Read and share this book and the lessons it holds. And, not because I said so, but because "Mama said!"

Dr. Joan M. Prince
Assistant Chancellor to the Dean
University of Wisconsin, Milwaukee

Are you hindering or helping success?

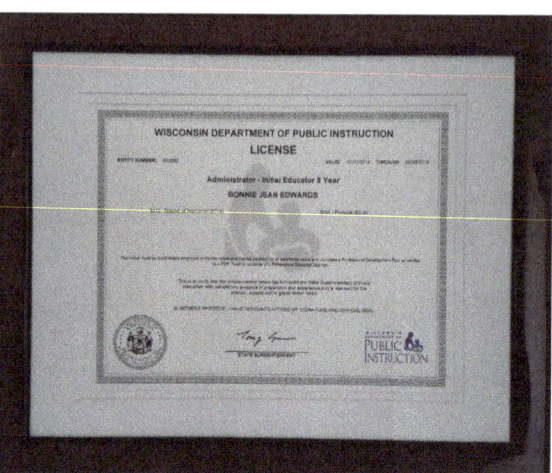

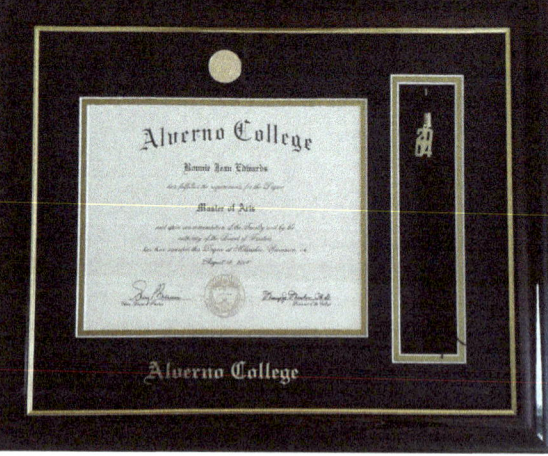

I'm Helping My Child By Supporting Positive Transformation

My Mother's High School
Graduation Photo

Bonnie's High School
Graduation Photo

Chapter 1

Mama's presence

It was another autumn day for students as they made their daily track at the end of the school day. The smothering temperatures reflecting from the freshly laid asphalt street sucked away the little bit of energy Bonita had as she approached home. Carrying a bundle of books only added additional stress to her petite physique as she struggled with each step. With a quick but short stride Bonita sprinted along her tree lined neighborhood flanked with brick tutor houses seeking refuge of the cool comfort of her own home.

"Hi Mama. I'm home."

Mama is in the kitchen as Bonita enters the front door. Bonita kicks off her shoes and toss her book bag down on the sun porch floor. She is met with a multitude of sun rays filtering through the front room of her home.

From a distance, mama's voice rings from the back of the house, "Hi Bonita, I'm in the kitchen."

Mama was always on Bonita about throwing her bags and jacket on the sunroom floor.

Mama would say, "Pick up your things and take them to your room where they belong."

Bonita's mother was very particular about the way the home was cared for. She loved a clean house and believed the home is where the heart is.

As Bonita picks up her books and bag, she reflects on her mother's words, "A cluttered house makes for an unhappy home."

"How was your day at school, Bonita?"

This question repeated itself everyday but it gave Bonita a sense of comfort just to hear it.

Mama's voice was like a song bird singing in a garden. In this moment the garden was the family kitchen and mama was nestled in the kitchen of her garden.

Bonita, a bright cheerful girl who loves being around her mother marches into the kitchen where mama is cooking her signature meal, golden fried chicken.

Bonita enters the kitchen yearning for mama's cooking, "Nobody fries chicken like you mama and you always made sure we have just enough."

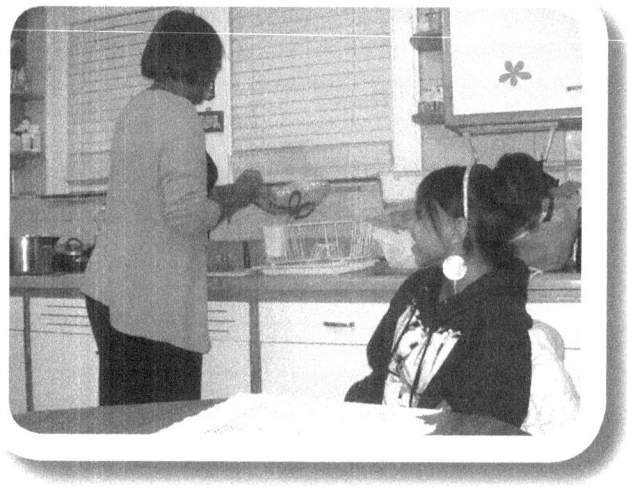

After gazing at the crisp chicken layered in the silver pan mama uses to drain the grease, Bonita hovers over the stove with anticipation, then she asks, "What's for desert?"

In a casual tone, Bonita lowered her head saying, "School was alright, mama." Bonita shows little enthusiasm for what happened in school today. She really enjoys school but not as much as she enjoys her friends. Her friends meant everything to her and it was not uncommon for Bonita to bring new friends home to meet her mother.

Bonita's mama would greet them with smiles and hugs as if they were her own. Mama's smiles were always warm and friendly so the neighborhood kids looked forward to visiting Bonita's house.

Mama didn't mind the kids from the neighborhood visiting as long as she was home to check them out. The scrutiny never bothered Bonita because she knew her mama enjoyed meeting her friends.

Bonita's mother asked, "What do you mean alright, Bonita?" With some reluctance, Bonita repeats herself, "It was alright."

"What did you learn in school?" asked mama.

"We learned a lot."

Bonita's response had the tone of evasiveness.

"Describe what you learned, Bonita?"

Bonita tries to change the subject.

"Mama it's hot in here. Why can't we get air conditioning?"

It was a hot autumn day and Bonita was already feeling worn out from her school day. Discussing school really wasn't what she wanted to do.

Bonita thought about her attitude for a moment and her conscience asked her, "How dare I give the impression to mama that I don't want to be bothered."

Bonita realizes she needs to get rid of her "Ms. It…plus a bag of chips" attitude. Bonita might have been naïve but she wasn't stupid. Bonita begins to reflect;

> *"…Mama believed in giving all of us a chance to talk about what was on our mind. Every once in a while I would find myself sitting at the kitchen table discussing the day's events with mama. Sometimes I had the nerve to complain about the time spent answering mama's questions but mama always remained calm and patient with me. I knew I had to open up and be honest about how my day went because Mama wasn't settling for less. I was always amazed at mama's ability to be there to listen to me and my other six siblings. We are really blessed to have a mother like mama."*

With a refreshed appreciation for mama's concern, Bonita walks into the sun porch and reaches for her book bag. She begins to pull out her math assignment.

Mama inquires, "What do you have there Bonita?"

Bonita pulls out a notebook with markings all over it. There are a slew of loose papers turned in every direction. Bonita navigates through her book bag finally reaching the heaviest of the many books, that would be a huge math book. This would not be Bonita's favorite subject.

Surprised by Bonita's book bag, her mother asks, "Good Lord Bonita, have you no sense of organization?"

Bonita's expression cracks a smile while she is amused, Bonita agrees with her mother's assessment.

"We worked on science, reading, writing, and oh, math." It all appeared to be a cluttered mess to Bonita's mother.

"Where is your home work?"

"It's right here."

Mama was persistent, "What are you suppose do tonight?"

"Math."

Bonita's mother felt her answer wasn't complete.

"Don't you think you need to get to work on it?"

"Yes mama," Bonita replies with a descending tone while clenching her teeth.

"Mama, I'm going to be honest. I don't get it."

"Get what?"

"This math stuff."

Bonita's mother is looking a bit puzzled.

"I can see you are tired and you seem to be stressing out about this homework assignment, Bonita."

"Mama, I am stressing."

Bonita shows frustration, "I don't get it!"

"I'm never going to get it."

"Calm down Bonita and take a deep breath." There is a pause in the conversation.

Bonita sat quietly at the table for a moment, she began to finger through her notes while contemplating on how to deal with all this homework.

As Bonita lifted her head, Thomas enters the kitchen, "Hey, twin sis, what's up?"

Thomas' diction always had a slang tone about it. He is so cool and compassionate about his twin sister. He shows genuine concern for her. When Bonita is not feeling well, Thomas suddenly feels bad too. Clearly annoyed, Bonita responds, "This math assignment!"

Thomas steps closer to Bonita. She is sitting across from her mother. Mama is patiently looking on as Thomas rolls up his sleeves and takes his seat in the brightly lit kitchen next to Bonita.

Thomas looks at Bonita and offers her a bit of home grown wisdom.

"Bonita,"You know that mama will always say, you get out of life what you put into life."

Bonita looks puzzled.

"What are you talking about Thomas?"

Thomas continues, "If you work hard at it with the right attitude, you will get it."

Bonita asks Thomas, "What do you mean about attitude?" Thomas sat in silence.

"I'm not upset Thomas, I just don't understand my math assignment." Mama chimes in.

"Thomas don't worry about Bonita right now. You concentrate on your homework too. LeAnn will help Bonita."

"Remember, you get out of life what you put into it. Keep an open mind Bonita, trust me. You got this."

Thomas listens to mama and slowly strolls across the kitchen floor.

"Remember what mama said, you get out of life what you put in it."

With mama's back to him, Thomas grabs a chicken leg and exits the kitchen.

Mama and Bonita have taken ownership of the kitchen again.

Through the room, colorful daisies that were imprinted on the cabinet's appeared to blossom. Bonita's concentration would be interrupted by the thought that those daisies appeared to be dancing right off the canvas of the kitchen cabinets.

"Bonita, are you listening?"

"Yeah mama, I mean yes mama, I'm listening."

"Well, it's time to get to work."

"I don't get math."

"What part of math don't you get Bonita?"

"All of it, mama."

Mama repeated herself.

"Well, LeAnn can help."

"Do I have to?" Bonita sighs.

Bonita engages in an extended conversation with mama about her homework.

"Yes, you have to get your school work done because your teacher will be expecting it tomorrow. Bonita, let me tell you something. Thomas made a good point about the importance of getting out of life what you put into it. Do you understand what Thomas was saying to you?"

"Yes, mama, but why does homework come so easy to LeAnn and everybody else. But I feel like I'm the only one struggling.

"The only thing that's worse than a failure is not trying," mama said.

"Thomas was saying to me that if I tried harder with the right attitude, I will get it."

"That's right, Bonita. It is normal to get frustrated over your homework assignment especially if you don't understand it. But if you continue to tell yourself, I can't do this you won't do it. But if you say to yourself, I think I can, what do you think might happen Bonita?"

"I might get it, mama?" Bonita began to feel the spirit of her mothers wisdom.

"Yes, Bonita. So don't give up on yourself. Keep an open mind. remember what your Daddy always says, "Once you get your education, you got it. No one can take it from you!"

Mama continued to cook facing the kitchen sink where Bonita is sitting with contentment while gazing at her mother washing the dishes, "Mama, I'm glad we talked about my assignment. I feel like I matter now."

Bonita mother's presence affirmed for Bonita that her mother enjoyed the conversation and that Bonita's feelings did matter to her.

Bonita shuffled through her Eighth grade papers. She gathered them and heads toward the living room. With books in hand, Bonita flops on the living room floor. The gold plush carpet cushions her as she lands flat on her backside. The comfort of the floor puts Bonita in a reflective mood;

> *"I have the entire space to me for now, that is until the rest of the family comes home. But for now, I have full claim to the living and dining room, most importantly, I have the undivided attention of mama. When my younger bothers (they are twins too), Randy and Andy come home they will get the attention from mama too. But mama is so good to us; we don't even realize whose getting more or less attention.*
>
> *Mama makes all of us feel like we're number one. She takes time for each one of us. We don't have reason to bicker and fight because we all feel important in mama's eyes. I wonder if all my friends get that kind of attention from their mama.*
>
> *When daddy comes home he makes us feel important too. Most times he is tired after working hard all day. His feet are tired and worn when he comes home after standing on his feet all day and night at the brewery."*
>
> *"Grab my bucket" daddy would say.*
> *"Put some hot water in it as hot as I can stand it."*

One of us, whom ever is in eyeshot of daddy runs to the bathroom like we were in a competition vying for his attention and approval. One of us grabs the bucket and runs the water as hot as he can stand it, and the lucky one cautiously takes the blue bucket loaded with water – splashing along the way.

Daddy is patiently waiting to soak his tired, worn feet. Most times he is either sitting at the edge of his bed or sitting in his smooth beige lazy boy chair that both he and mama shared.

Chapter 2

A time for learning

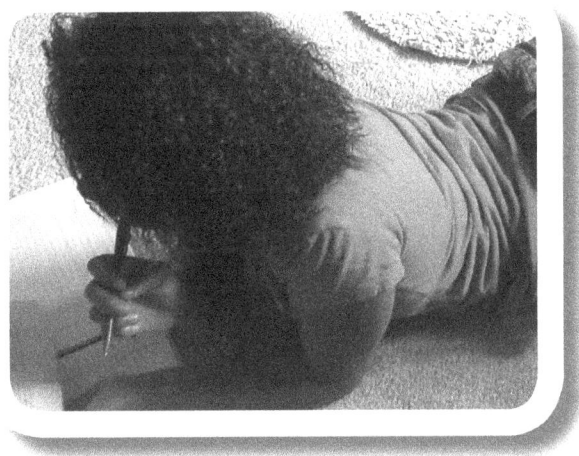

For now, Bonita has free reign of the house. That's the way she prefers it, quiet with a feeling of solitude. Bonita lay on the floor indecisive about which homework to tackle first. She takes a moment to stare through the French doors that separated the sunroom from the living room. Without any real reason Bonita begins looking from right to left marveling at the many windows that seem to stand in unison like soldiers saluting all who enter her fortress. The front door opens with a squeak and through the leaded glass a voice emerges from the silence.

"Hey, mama!"

Bonita is still spawned across the living room floor.

From the kitchen, you can hear mama's voice, "Hey, LeAnn."

LeAnn addresses Bonita.

"Why are you stretched out across the living room floor when you could be sitting at the dining room table working on your homework?"

LeAnn is four years older than Bonita.

Bonita is taken aback by LeAnn's question and continues to focus on her homework.

Suddenly, Bonita realizes her private claim to mama and having the house to herself has been interrupted. Shortly, the living room floor will be the pathway for more footsteps, the sofa will not look so neat, and the firm pillows will be tossed about. Loud noises will vibrate from the television console. The perfect stream of sunlight passing through the colored leaded glass windows will soon fade.

"LeAnn is that you?"

Mama shouted from the sweltering kitchen. The aroma and imminent taste of golden crisp chicken teases LeAnn's palette.

"Yea, mama it's me."

Making her way to the back of the house, "It smells good in here. What are you cooking, mama?"

Mama responds to LeAnn.

"How was your day at school, LeAnn?"

"We practiced our drill and I came up with some new techniques. Everybody seemed to like it. It was hard but we had fun."

LeAnn is a drill team captain at Washington High. She is a popular student and sharp as a razor. Her friends enjoy hanging out with her. She enjoys learning. LeAnn is truly a born leader. More than that, she is known as "Big Sis" and take her role seriously. She is the only one in the house that gets to have her own room. She has earned that spot because she is Big Sis.

Bonita reflects on a moment she had with her sister, LeAnn. She remembers the one time mama asked LeAnn to comb her hair.

Bonita reflects on that fateful day,

> "I could have gone the whole day without having my hair combed. My hair was short and soft. Mama always says, I'm tender headed. I didn't have much hair so I wanted to keep the little bit I did have."

Everybody knows you don't mess with "Big Sis." Bonita's parents relied on LeAnn a lot when they were not at home. She had a huge responsibility. As the eldest child, LeAnn had the responsibility of helping to see to it that the others followed the house rules and there were many. Some rules were easy to comply with like no company in the house when mama and daddy were not at home. Other rules were more challenging to comply with like coming straight home from school. We were expected to follow the rules, LeAnn was the enforcer.

Everyone in the house has strong personalities. My big sister LeAnn, is amazing! She is smart, fun to be around and loved her younger brothers and sisters. Cal is the next in charge. He has the reputation of being a lady's man and he is quite the athlete. Cal was happiest when he was hanging out with his friends. His 1980 Monty Carlo with its big white walls and chrome rims always announced his arrival.

All of Bonita's brothers are athletic. Bonita's twin brother Thomas has a love for football. He is fast, furious and strong. Everyday you can find him throwing the football to his neighborhood friends in front of the house. Thomas had a strong arm. He would throw bombs nearly all the way to the end of the street leaving his friends in disbelief.

The younger twins are built for basketball. Both of them played in some version of a basketball league. Most times many of their friends gravitated to the house just to hang out with Andy and randy.

Clarisa is the most quiet of all of Bonita's siblings but all so talented. She is an amazing artist and sometimes she would reveal her talents to the family by illustrating her unique fashions in her art portfolio. Clarisa knew fashion.

"Your sister needs your help with her home work," mama said to Le Ann.

Bonita is lying on the floor feeling overwhelmed by all the work. "Where's everybody, mama?"

"Your dad is working at the business, the boys are playing ball down the street, Cal is at football practice and Clarisa, and Thomas are watching television downstairs."

LeAnn sits down on the floor with Bonita and proceeds to look at her assignments.

"I don't understand any of this!" says Bonita.

"I'll help you understand. Let's sit at the dining room table. The light over there is better. Look at this math problem. What are they asking you to do?"

"Well, I think subtract this number from this number."

"Not quite, read the problem."

"I don't understand what they are asking me to do."

"Bonita, look at the problem. If you took this from this, what's left?"

"I don't know!"

"It's right there in front of you." LeAnn appears irritated.

LeAnn is not having any luck with Bonita. She gets impatient and Bonita shuts down. Mama enters the living room from the kitchen and sits down in her lazy chair.

"Mama I tried! Bonita's brains must be wired differently. She can't seem to concentrate."

"Bonita, what's the problem, mama asks?"

Bonita quietly returned to the floor. She is met by mama's reassuring voice.

"Bonita, God never said life would be easy. We will have good and bad days."

"I don't get it, mama!"

Mama focused in on Bonita's body language. She knew that Bonita had difficulties expressing herself at times when she is frustrated about something.

Is there something else on your mind you want to talk about?" asked mama.

"This assignment is difficult."

"What do you mean this assignment is difficult?"

"All we do in class is sit in our seats and listen to the teacher."

"Bonita, you are in school to learn and not to play."

"But, mama! You don't understand!"

"Bonita I understand that this is a problem for you. But, what I don't understand is why this math has you so upset."

Bonita is feeling discouraged and says to her mother, "Nobody understands me."

"That may be true," Mama said, "but believe it or not you do have some control over your situation, Bonita."

Chapter 3

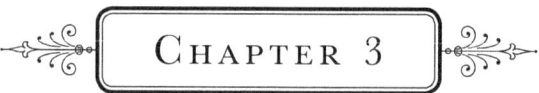
Mama checks in

At this point Mama knew she had to break it down to Bonita's level to help her understand her situation better.

Mama starts a dialog with Bonita.

"Remember last Sunday in church during Pastor Glory's sermon, you grabbed my arm when Ms. Hallie jumped up from her seat screaming, hollering and waving her hands right before that beautiful hat she was wearing flew across the pew?"

"Yes, mama I remember and I was worried about her. She is always so nice to me."

Mama often used stories to explain big and small problems to Bonita.

"Ms. Hallie is one of the elders in church who always appear cool and calm not to mention, every Sunday she wears such beautiful clothes."

"Yes, she usually does."

"Mama I've never seen Ms. Hallie wear the same suit or hat. She must have a closet full of clothes like you mama."

"Bonita, remember last Sunday you became afraid because you thought Ms. Hallie was having a nervous breakdown?"

"But she really wasn't?"

"Yea."

"During Pastor Glory's sermon, Ms. Hallie felt the Holy Spirit come over her and she let out a joyful noise!"

"She looked like she was crying."

Pastor Glory's powerful message about God's love filled her heart to the point that she had to let it out."

"She sure did mama."

At this point Mama knew she had Bonita's attention, "Bonita, when you know God is in your heart, it is in that moment you know God is speaking to you through the pastor. It's a moment Ms. Hallie will cherish forever. Now, in case you are wondering what does Ms. Hallie's experience have to do with your math assignment, well Bonita, you didn't understand what was happening to Ms. Hallie last Sunday in church right?"

"No mama, I didn't."

"Did you feel better when you understood what was happening to her?"

"Yea, mama."

Why did you feel better about Ms. Hallie, Bonita?"

"I felt better mama because I knew Ms. Hallie was going to be alright."

"That's right Bonita," Mama said, "like your math assignment, once you understand it, you won't be afraid of it and you will be alright too."

"Wow mama, when you put it that way it does make me feel a little better."

At this point Bonita looked at her math in a whole new light.

Mama continued to share some of her own personal stories with Bonita.

"I remember struggling in math too."

"Really, mama?"

"In fact, English was my favorite subject. When I didn't understand my math, I asked a lot of questions."

"What kind of questions mama?"

"I remember one day I was struggling and no one was home to help me when I needed it. Being the eldest child, my little brothers and sisters looked up to me all the time."

While sitting in the family living room, Bonita's mother continues to reminisce as Bonita listens on.

"Daddy was busy working on the farm and my mother had the little ones to tend to. I had to rely a lot on myself."

Times were so hard for Bonita's mother back in the day. Grandpa Lil had to manage the farm and harvest the land. There was never a boring day for Grandpa Lil.

Mama continued to reveal her story.

"I remember praying to God for electricity so that I can use an iron to care for my clothes. We needed electricity not just for ironing but for light. Imagine doing your homework in the dark?"

"No, that would be hard," Bonita said, "I'm glad our lights are on mama. But, it wouldn't be such a bad thing either. This way I wouldn't have to think about doing my home work." Bonita says with a smirk.

Mama sighs and chuckles, showing her dimples as she engages Bonita in her story.

"But getting back to my story, Bonita, I knew school was a place I could get help with my assignments. So I asked a lot of questions when I didn't understand something. You have to learn how to do that too Bonita."

Bonita responds, "I can't imagine not having any lights on in the house."

Mama said, "Bonita, promise me that you will go to school tomorrow and ask one question to your teacher."

"Yes, I promise, mama. What am I asking for?"

"Bonita, ask Ms. Williams if she can help you understand your math homework? I guarantee you she will gladly help you."

"She has so many other students that need help and she won't have time to help me."

With a compassionate voice Mama responded, "If she cares about you Bonita, she will help you. Pray for help Bonita and help will come."

"Mama, my teacher is nice but sometimes she has to yell because some of the kids don't listen to directions. That puts her in a bad mood."

Mama explained, "Bonita, you have to believe that you deserve to be helped like any other student. You are worthy of help. Don't you think you deserve help?"

Trusting and believing in mama, Bonita had to agree, "I guess so mama."

"Bonita, keep this in mind," Bonita's mother goes on to say, "It's the small victories that count."

"If I can understand my assignment mama, it would be a victory!"

"All you need to do is take this problem one step at a time. You must believe you will get help if you just ask."

Mama reminds Bonita, "remember what your dad says," Bonita interrupts, "I know mama…once you get your education no one can take it from you."

"Right!"

After this conversation, Bonita felt a sense of relief but there was still one thing puzzling her.

"By the way mama, how long did you go without electricity?"

"It wasn't too long Bonita. God answered my prayers. We moved into a home with electricity! I prayed and prayed and I believed our situation would improve in due time."

Bonita, picking up her book bag, heads toward the stairs with a little more pep in her step, climbs the stairs where she shares a bedroom with her sister Clarisa. The room is small but big enough for the two of them. Bonita, her twin brother and Clarisa are just one year apart.

Bonita's sister is blessed with an artistic eye. She is highly intelligent and gets straight A's in school. Bonita enjoys sharing the story about the times when Clarisa took her to the public swimming pool. It was there that Clarisa taught Bonita how to swim.

The sun has set. The night has arrived. Bonita lay in bed staring at the ceiling of her dark room. She closed her eyes and thought deeply about her conversation with her mother. Bonita reflects;

> *"Mama said, keep an open mind, don't be afraid to ask questions and to remember it's the small victories that count."*

Chapter 4

A problem is solved

It's a new day! On an early Tuesday morning the sun was shining through Bonita's bedroom curtains serving as a lamp for the beginning of a bright day. "Bonita, Randy, Thomas, David, hurry up, get down here and eat!"

This ritual was echoed out each morning by Bonita's mother.

Bonita grabbed the hot egg sandwich her mother prepared for her. Seasoned just right, the scrambled egg sandwich was always fluffy and each bite would melt inside her mouth. The cold glass of milk was the fuel that gave her the energy to start another challenging day.

The lights were still dim in Mama's and Daddy's bedroom. Bonita taps on the cracked door, opens it wide enough that her soft voice could stream through.

"Mama, I'm leaving for school."

Bonita reaches over the night stand to get her bus and lunch money.

"Did you eat?"

"Yes."

Most times the bus and lunch money is waiting for Bonita and her brothers in neatly organized stacks on the night stand.

Bonita and Thomas went out the front door down the concrete steps of the front porch, running to catch the bus. Most times, Bonita was running behind Thomas. He was fast. Sure enough the bus would arrive within seconds.

The twins walked to Garden Homes Elementary School in the neighborhood. They had a lot of energy to burn off so walking was good for them. Their friends would ring the doorbell before they could even get their tennis shoes tied up.

The school wasn't that far, maybe six blocks.

Bonita and Thomas caught the city bus. It wasn't Bonita's favorite part of the day. She met some of her classmates on the bus at the point of transfer on Center and 27th Street.

Mama said...It's the small victories that count!

The bus ride comprised of the two busiest streets on the north side of the city. Like in most large urban cities, most of the African Americans students lived on a certain side of town. For Bonita, it was the North side. Bonita and Thomas were always happy to see some of their classmates as they arrive at school on their way to room 146. The students are coming in from all directions.

Greg is chasing Mark down the hallway despite the "No running in the Hallway" sign posted along the narrow corridor.

Danielle and Julia are just turning the corner swapping lip gloss. Hosea is speed walking toward the classroom trying to race against the first bell.

Hosea is speed walking toward the classroom trying to race against the first bell.

Niah, one of the smartest girls in the class is strolling into the classroom smiling at Ms. Williams as she enters.

"Good morning everyone."

"Hi Ms. Williams."

Ms. Williams stands majestically at the classroom doorway.

"Hello to you Julius."

Bonita reflects in this moment,

> *"Julius is a popular student at Brighton Academy. He thinks all the girls like him and actually he's not bad looking when he combs his hair. Sometimes he wears dreads and other times he wears his hair natural. I try to ignore him like the plague as he passes by me in the hallway, "Wass up, Bonita?" with a silly smirk on his face. I ignore him and I keep walking. I make a bee line to my buddy Simone who I see walking with a group of other girls down the hall."*

At the classroom door students continued to enter.

Ms. Williams remains patient as the remaining students enter the classroom. She stands tall and slender with a graceful statue. She is firm yet gentle with her students. Ms. Williams demeanor commands respect from those who was fortunate enough to know her. She respects her students, even the ones who are disrespectful. Her students respect her. Ms. Williams colleagues seek her out when they need advice on lesson planning or classroom management. Parents know her to be a good listener, resourceful and fair with her students.

"Ms. Williams, guess what happened to me yesterday?"

"What happened Julius?"

Ms. Williams played along with his Q & A.

"I beat my big brother Edward in a chess game."

Julius is proud and feels he has earned his bragging rights for beating his "BIG" brother in a game of chess.

Ms. Williams appeared pleasantly surprised, "Well, good for you Julius."

"I'm the king…I'm the king…" echoed Julius as he distanced himself into the classroom.

An abrupt message resonates over the loud speaker.

"One of the school buses assigned to the school is running a tad late, teachers please do not mark students tardy."

This is a common occurrence at Brighton Academy.

Bonita grabs her math book from her locker anticipating Ms. Williams reaction about her missing math assignment while also thinking about the conversation she had with her mother the night before.

"Come in everyone and take your assigned seats."

"By groups, please turn in your math assignments." Suddenly, Bonita is feeling sick to her stomach.

"Ms. Williams may I have permission to go to the bathroom?"

Mama said...It's the small victories that count!

    Ms. Williams doesn't hear Bonita speaking from her desk. Bonita raises her hand but Ms. Williams doesn't see or hear her because she's busy taking attendance and tallying lunch count.

    Sounding a bit more demanding, Bonita blurts out, "Ms. Williams, Ms. Williams, may I please go to the bathroom?"

    Ms. Williams is surprised by the outburst but acknowledges her.

    "Bonita you just arrived, you know the rules no bathroom breaks before 9:00 a.m."

    "But it's an emergency, Ms. Williams."

    "Of course go ahead Bonita, take the bathroom pass with you please."

Chapter 5

Bonita's transformation

Bonita leaps from her desk like a jack rabbit on burning coal. She dashes out of the room, races down the hall, burst into the bathroom, and then reaches into her jacket pocket pulling out her math assignment. She fights to hold back her whaling tears.

"What is wrong with me?" Bonita is thinking.

The neatly folded math assignment is now moist and stained from her dripping tears. Bonita digs deep into her emotions to compose herself.

"O.k, be a big girl, Bonita," she attempts to uplift herself.

Once she gets it together Bonita makes her way back to the classroom. Upon entering the room, Bonita sense that she is the focus of classroom snickering.

Bonita is not aware that there are squares of bathroom tissue attached to the bottom of one of her tennis shoes.

Capturing the attention of her friend, Bonita, whispering, "What?" Only Simone offers Bonita a feeling of friendly support.

One of her classmates Julius yells out, "She has toilet paper stuck on the bottom of her shoe!"

The entire classroom erupts into uncontrollable laughter. Bonita is instantly covered with a blanket of embarrassment.

Reaching the top of her voice, Ms. Williams tells the class, "Calm down and refocus please!"

After the excitement at Bonita's expense, Ms. Williams started the math lesson. Ms. Williams takes the bundle of math assignments from her homework tray and begins calling off students' names.

She asks everyone whose name was called to stand up at their desk. This was one of her ways of recording her students' progress and participation.

The students stood up one by one near their desks as requested but Bonita remained sitting.

Bonita is feeling a bit queasy and awkward.

"Everyone sit down," said Ms. Williams.

The students sat down. Ms. Williams directs the students, "Continue with today's assignment on the board first, then copy the problem, and try to work on the problem by yourselves for five minutes."

"Awhh," as the students began to grumble. They were not happy. The students wanted to partner with their buddies.

"Afterwards, join your partners when you have completed the problem on your own. Does anyone have any questions?"

In unison, all the students responded with a chorus of "no" Ms. Williams."

"Bonita, would you come up to my desk please?"

Bonita was afraid. She didn't come prepared. She didn't budge. With her petite and doll like features she sat firmly in her chair.

"Bonita, I asked you to come up to speak with me regarding your homework assignment."

Ms. Williams sits at her desk waiting patiently for Bonita to approach her desk.

Bonita raises her small frame slowly and walks timidly up the aisle. Along the way, she passes her buddy Simone who gives her a funny look as she approaches Ms. Williams's desk.

"Why did it take you so long to come to me Bonita?"

"Ms Williams, I already felt bad about not having my assignment in. I felt worse when you had everybody who completed their assignment stand up. I was the only one sitting down."

"I'm sorry you felt bad but you know this is our procedure."

"Don't you want to be acknowledged too when you complete your homework Bonita?"

With a whimpering voice, "Do we have to stand Ms. Williams?"

"Believe it or not Bonita; it helps me just like it helps you and the rest of the class. It allows me to immediately see who is getting their home work done and it keeps me organized too!"

"Why didn't you complete your homework assignment last night Bonita?

"I tried Ms. Williams and my big sister LeAnn tried to help me too and I still couldn't get it."

Bonita's classmates are engaging in small talk with their peers while Bonita continues to consult with her teacher. Her hands are feeling sweaty and her eyes are beginning to whale up again. She is getting upset and feeling a little embarrassed by what she sees as unfair criticism.

"Calm down and relax Bonita. I will help you and we will figure this out together."

"Ms. Williams, mama told me that I should ask questions when I don't understand something."

"Explain what you mean, Bonita."

"Well, I didn't understand my math homework so I didn't turn my assignment in. Mama told me I should ask you for help."

"Oh, I see, Bonita."

At this point, Bonita is beginning to feel a little more confident in her ability to express herself. With her mother's blessings and her teacher's encouragement, Bonita speaks openly.

"Can you help me, Ms. Williams?"

"Of course, I can, Bonita."

Ms. Williams reaches across her desk and turns toward her brown wooden book shelf and places a huge book in front of Bonita.

"This book is for Teachers Bonita. But in this book I have similar problems you have in your book."

"Ms. Williams, your book cover looks like my book cover."

"That's right, Bonita. But my book will help me help you understand your mathematics better."

"How does it work, Ms. Williams?" Ms. Williams interjects.

"Class, return to your assigned seats and write a one page summary about your discussions regarding your math problems."

Julius, leading the pack, "Do we have to, Ms. Williams?"

"Yes, everybody must follow instructions."

The students playfully return to their seats.

Ms. Williams tells the students to, "Write clearly and with complete sentences. Don't forget to watch your grammar."

Ms. Williams turns back toward Bonita. Bonita is concentrating on every word coming from her teacher.

Ms. Williams looks into Bonita's curious eyes and shares with her a word problem that was part of her homework lesson.

"Do you want to know about two strategies that I think will help you with this assignment, Bonita?"

Bonita is squirming in her seat next to Ms. Williams. She is also gazing around the classroom watching her peers work. It appears that some of them are smiling back at her too.

Bonita, re-enters the dialog, "Yes, Ms. Williams!"

"Bonita, it's easy. All you have to do is remember to read the directions and then you will understand. Ask yourself these four important questions on any mathematics assignment…"

1. Who is in the word problem and what is their role?
2. Does the problem want me to add, subtract, multiply, or divide?
3. What is the word problem asking me to do?
4. Where can I find the best possible answer?

Ms. Williams reiterated, remember to explain how you got your answer.

"Ms. Williams, you mean I just need to ask myself these four simple questions when I'm solving a math problem?"

"Yes, Bonita. It is just that simple." The classroom telephone rings.

"Hello," Ms. Williams answers with a polite and friendly tone.

"Hello, is this Ms. Williams?

"Yes, it is. May I help you?"

"Yes, this is Bonita Gladney's mother. I hope I am not disturbing you too much."

"No, not at all, I'm glad you called."

"I asked Bonita to see you this morning for help with her math assignment. Did she come to you for help?"

"Oh yes, we were just working on it together."

A big sigh came over the telephone from Bonita's mother. You could feel her excitement.

"Dear Lord, thank you Ms. Williams for taking time with Bonita. She was really stressing over this last night."

Ms. Williams shared her plan with Bonita's mother, "Today, I offered her some tips on what to do when she encounters an assignment she doesn't understand."

"Great! I was no help to her last night. Math was never my favorite subject. I even had her oldest sister LeAnn help her."

"No problem. Feel free to call me anytime, said Ms. Williams. We have other resources for Bonita too. Are you interested in knowing about our after school tutoring program?"

"Oh yes!"

"Well, no problem. I'll send information home with Bonita tonite to share with you."

Bonita's mother felt relieved.

"Thank you again for everything, Ms. Williams."

"Is there anything else I can help you with Ms. Gladney?"

"You've done enough, Thank you."

Bonita was anxiously waiting for Ms. Williams to hang up the phone. She didn't know her teacher was talking to her mother.

"Ms. Williams, while you were on the telephone, I tried to work on the problem by myself. Did I get it right?"

She looked over Bonita's word problem and placed her paper down gently, lifts up her right hand and with excitement gives Bonita a big high-five.

Bonita responds with excitement!

"I DID it!"

Bonita is a good dancer and wasn't shy about displaying her new found confidence. Bonita and Ms. Williams celebrated her accomplishment by dancing in step together. She has achieved a huge task. The other students were cheering her on too.

Bonita returns to her seat and proceeds with getting her work done. twenty minutes later, Ms. Williams dismisses the students to their next class. On the way out the door, Bonita's buddy Simone cornered her.

"How did you do that?"

Bonita said, "Do what?"

"How did you solve the math problem?"

Bonita said to Simone, "Don't you know, after all, you stood up when your name was called."

"Yeah, but that didn't mean I understood the homework assignment." Simone smirked.

Bonita looking puzzled, "Simone, I thought you and the whole class understood the assignment."

Simone paused then replied, "Well, I can only speak for myself, raising her voice, "I still need help."

"Simone, I thought I was all alone."

"Can you help me Bonita like Ms. Williams helped you?"

"Sure I can Simone. I will help you under one condition."

"What?" Simone asked.

"Girl, my mama said, 'It's the small victories that count.' So the first victory is you got to ask the question. You can't be afraid to ask the question if you don't understand something. Believe me, this was a small victory for me! I'm free to ask questions without feeling embarrassed. Think about it, once we get our education, can't nobody take it away from us. It's in us for life."

Bonita shares a bag of Planters peanuts with her friend and grabs Simone's arm. Like best friends they walk down the hallway to their next class. Like girls sometimes do, they proceed to their next class giggling along the way and teasing each other.

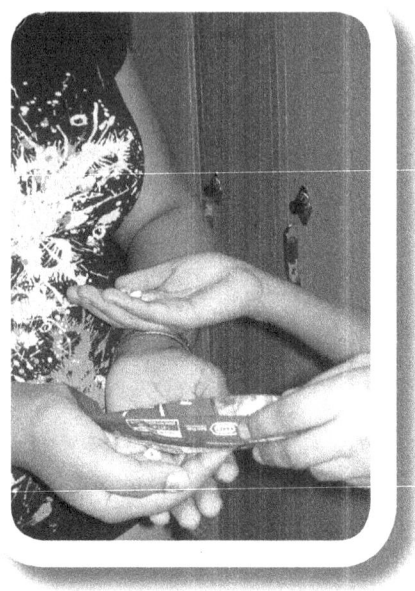

Simone breaks away from Bonita's arm, both of them begin chasing each other and laughing along the way disregarding the sign posted on the school walls, "No running in the Hallway."

Chapter 6

A sense of Pride

Bonita's arrives home from school. The aroma of her mother's kitchen meets her at the door.

"Hi mama, I have some exciting news."

"What is it, Bonita?"

Bonita is speaking with new confidence, "Mama, I did what you told me to do, I asked my teacher for help with my math assignment."

"You did?" Bonita's mother was pleased.

Bonita has more excitement in her voice, "Yes mama."

"Ms. Williams had the class work on an assignment while she sat me down near her desk. She gave me tips on how to work the problem. While Ms. Williams was on the phone I had to figure it out for myself and I did!"

Bonita had no idea that it was her mom Ms. Williams was speaking to on the telephone.

"Well mama, I had to believe I could do it. I remembered what Thomas told me about my attitude. So I thought about what he said. Mama when I changed the way I was looking at my assignments the work became easier just like Thomas said!

You said it is the small victories that count. Asking the question was the victory for me, wasn't it mama?"

Bonita's mother is full of pride, "I'm proud of you and I love you Bonita. I am most proud that you reached an understanding of not just your assignment, but of yourself. You did this. Not I, Thomas or LeAnn. You did!"

Inspired and feeling more hopeful, Bonita inquires about the after school tutoring program.

"Mama when can I start the after-school tutoring program?"

Well, according to these forms you brought home, you can start as soon as I sign these papers. With a bit of humor, Bonita responds, "Can we eat first?" Both Bonita and her mother smiles and embrace each other with a hug.

My mother always said...
"Believe In Yourself"

Bonnie J. Edwards

5 Ws Mama said...
"It's the small victories that count."
The Communication Companion - Born To Succeed!
(A personal guide and a constant resource for all audiences)

Who - Students; parents; educators; administrators; staff
What - The Communication Companion; A Student's Motivational and Inspirational Tool
Where - The Communication Companion can be used anywhere anytime - (school, home, play, extra-curricular activities, clubs, home-schooling, private/public school instruction)
When - Can be used during instructional day/before/during/after school/at home.
Why - The Communication Companion helps individuals (students, educators and parents focus on the current moment of a child's development) become reflective and more self-aware.
How - The Communication Companion can inspire, motivate students as well as encourage educators and parents to guide student intellectual and emotional development. The guide helps students take ownership of their own personal and intellectual growth.

"Mama said..."

Be a cool, calm, confident communicator
The Communication Companion
Be inspired by Mama's pearls of wisdom sprinkled with
communication, love, compassion and family

Third Edition

"Mama said..."

Be the Cool, Calm and Confident Communicator (CCCCs)

A Communication Companion

A young carefree teenager by the name of Bonita, like most teenagers, is playful, loves adventure and loves playing with her friends. She tells the story about how her mother helped her overcome some amazing challenges. But when she is met with the challenges of school and maturing into her teens, she leans on her mother's pearls of wisdom. Bonita learns how to overcome her challenges. Her mother sprinkled her wisdom, love and compassion transforming Bonita into a cool, calm, and confident communicator.

When open communication is valued in homes and in schools it can make a world of difference in the way people get along and communicate with each other. In this narrative, you will see how the pearls of wisdom Bonita's mother created was a loving pathway for meaningful and brighter relationships at home and in school.

Be the Cool, Calm and Confident Communicator

"Mama said..."

"It's the small victories that count."

Introduction

One of the most memorable conversations I had with my mother before she passed concerned pursuing a career in teaching. She believed my disposition and attitude regarding teaching children was perfect and came natural to me. My mother knew my temperament, compassion and my ability to communicate effectively with others. One year later, thanks to my mother's pearls of wisdom the opportunity presented itself.

    A couple of years after my conversation with my mother, I studied and became a licensed middle school teacher. The first year of teaching in an urban school environment presented me with unimaginable challenges. It was in this moment I began to question if going into teaching was the right direction for me. The passion was there, what was in question was whether or not the stamina was there. Fourteen years later, and completing two successful graduate programs including Certification in Administrative Leadership and Director of Instruction, along with developing curriculum for graduate courses in Continuing Education, including participating in Advance Doctoral Studies, I left the public sphere of teaching to accompany my husband, Cary who had recently retired himself with 40 years in television broadcasting. After retirement, time and space opened up for me to pursue my vocation as a writer, something I've always wanted to do as long as I can remember. Who would have thought that the blessing would come in the form of celebrating my mother's legacy. I've had many reflections about my practice as an educator. Those reflections always came back around to my mother, resting on this one thought, "If I could only talk to my mother."

While teaching in public education for more than a decade, I observed many issues facing students, parents, and educators. The problems were not insurmountable. However, the common denominator was poor communication skills. Pure, home grown communication was absent. For each negative experience encountered only propelled me to explore positive experiences during my tenure. If only I could talk to my mother. I knew my mother had the answers. Clearly, the students, adults, and the professionals needed an intervention. I wondered, would they be open to developing new communication skills if given the opportunity?

The opportunity materialized. I knew the task at hand could not be resolved by waving a magic wand. This mission would require all stakeholders to be on board working together. The mission began with a fresh set of eyes on building a different type of curriculum. A curriculum that could be used by new and veteran educators in any school district. It is true that it takes two or more individuals to communicate. These educators would discover their existing and preferred communication styles.

This new communication curriculum would offer a reliable and sustainable framework for practicing educators or for anyone interested in promoting positive relationships. These models are research-based and provides clear explanation for human motivation and behavior.

The first model, Maslow Hierarchy of Needs on human motivation is well established in educational, health and business communities.

The second model, Johari Window on self-awareness is somewhat new to educational communities. Its impact is huge. This model provides a window for open and positive communication practices for individuals who want to improve in their communication skills personally and professionally.

The third model is rooted in Block's community; A Structure of Belonging. Peter Block, an author and researcher coined what it means to create communities that have a structure of belonging.

He understands what it means to hold stakeholders accountable, even in school settings. His timely and classic approach to building and sustaining communities aligns well with the previous modalities mentioned. Block illustrates how families and the education communities should work cohesively. We will discover how Block's process works as our discussion continues.

These three communication models helps to understand the story of "Mama Said…" as well as the Communication Companion.

The following chapters will examine how the story "Mama Said…" has laid the foundation for improved communication across families, students and school communities.

It is important to note that in the story, "Mama Said…" Bonita's mother completed formal high school at Utica Institute in Utica, Mississippi. Bonita's mother had much to offer. She did not study scientists who specialized in socializing or human behavior. Clearly, if Bonita's mother would have had an opportunity to pursue college, imagine how many people would have been touched by her wisdom. This was not the case. However, it is possible that Bonita's mother, through personal and business experience came across studies in human behavior that were relatable to her at the time. It was her experience as a mother, wife, business women, spiritual advisor and coach that helped her realize her worth and contribution to her family and community. This allowed Bonita's mother to use that wisdom in rearing her children and touching the lives of others.

Bonita mother's priorities were with her family. Her knowledge came from her unwavering faith and love for her family. Her mother had the wisdom, vision and the compassion to build character in her children.

Bonita remembered how her mother engaged her one day at the dining room table. This was as new experience with Bonita together with her mother. Her mother invited her to participate in an activity. Bonita enjoyed it. Her mother used flash cards to get her to think about what she valued in life. Each card was labeled with different terms like education, prestige, wealth, vocation, or travel. Certainly, Bonita's mother had some knowledge of communication concepts.

This was even more apparent in how she balanced and managed her career and family. She used her business sense, knowledge, and people skills to build character in her children during their critical developmental years.

In the following chapters, three communication models are introduced to illustrate and explain these communication concepts. Bonita mother's 'pearl of wisdom' are embedded in each model. Each communication model will explain the family dynamics observed in the story. Applying the communication models here are applicable because in the story there is plenty of evidence that explains Bonita's mother's motivation on how open communication is the goal.

The goal here for "Mama Said…" is to help readers understand the importance of open communication and its positive impact on family relationships. Using these communication models will allow us to examine the usefulness of the models in family and school relationships.

"Mama said..."
A Communication Companion
Pearls of Wisdom

 **(1)** Maslow Hierarchy of Needs

 (2) Johari's Window

 (3) Block's Community: The Structure of Belonging

 **(1) Pearl of Wisdom**

Maslow Hierarchy of Needs

The first of the communication models examined is Maslow's Hierarchy of Needs by Abraham Maslow, a psychologist in human behavior. He is known for the popular Maslow Hierarchy of Needs pyramid. Maslow passed away in 1968. So much of his research (published and unpublished) was understood and celebrated by countless colleagues, universities, colleges, K-12, medical and business industries.

The pyramid illustrates how individuals are motivated in meeting their basic needs. These needs can range from getting proper nutritious meals to receiving positive mental stimulation in the home environment. This model is important and considered the first 'pearl of wisdom' illustrated in the story. Using Maslow allows you to see how Bonita's mother made sure that the basic needs of Bonita and the rest of her family were met.

The diagram below provides a good visual representation of many patterns of behaviors manifested in "Mama Said…" aligned with Maslow Hierarchy of Needs. Let's take a look.

Evidence of Maslow's Theory in "Mama Said…"

- When Bonita walks inside her home from school; She experiences: security; safety
- Bonita greets her mother in the kitchen; She experiences: food; shelter
- Bonita's mother acknowledges her; She experiences: love, belonging
- Bonita's mother listening to her frustrations and fears; She experiences: love, belonging, self-esteem, confidence
- Thomas, Bonita's brother offers his opinion; She experiences: love, belonging, confidence
- Bonita's one on one time with her mother: She experiences: love, belonging, self-esteem, confidence, security
- Bonita's tutoring sessions with LeAnn (eldest sister) She experiences: love, belonging, self-esteem
- Bonita's relationship with her friend, Simone. She experiences: belonging, self-esteem, self-actualization
- Bonita's relationship with Ms. Williams (Teacher) She experiences: safety, security, self-esteem, confidence, self-actualization
- Bonita's transformation: She experiences: security, safety, love, belonging, self-esteem, confidence, self-actualization
- Bonita knew that the only way she could overcome her fears about math was to face it. Bonita was shy. She also

had opinions about her fears. She appeared willing to acknowledge those fears enough to listen and trust her mother for guidance.
- She experiences: safety, security, self-esteem, confidence, self- actualization
- Bonita understood the importance of listening to her mother. She also knew that if there was going to be change, it would have to start with her believing in herself. She experiences: security, self- actualization

Maslow's Hierarchy of Needs

Maslow's research explained human motivation. When an individual's basic needs are met (e.g., food and water), the individual is then motivated to reach the next level in the hierarchy of needs. The illustration below provides a detailed explanation.

Motivational level   **Description of person at this level**

Table 1 Maslow Hierarchy of Needs

Self-transcendence	To have a peak experience beyond the boundaries of self
Self-actualization	To be fulfilled; doing what one was born to do
Esteem needs	Being recognized for some form of achievement
Belongingness and love	Strive for affiliation
Safety needs	Strive for safety and security
Physiological (survival) needs	Strive to secure the basic necessities of life (water, food)

This model is appropriate in examining the story, "Mama Said…" The concept aligns well with Bonita's relationship with her mother. Evidence of Maslow is defined and explained in Table 1.

It is important to note that a child experience will vary from family to family because an individual experience is unique for them in their family structure. Many of us can agree that family dynamics are multi-complicated and what may work for one family may not work for another family.

The experience of Bonita and her relationship with her mother applies in many families today. This "pearl of wisdom" represented by Maslow Hierarchy of Needs is a useful tool in any family structure.

When practiced under the right circumstances it can prove to be useful and meaningful in building strong family relationships. You will know the practice is working when you can observe transforming behaviors and attitudes taking place in the home and in the school community.

What I understand about his theory is how they manifested in Bonita's daily life at home. remember I said mama relied on her unwavering faith and love to raise healthy and well rounded children? Well, Bonita mother's parenting style worked for her. My hope is that you see the similarities and differences that impact motivation and behavior.

Bonita's mother did not rely on popular thought or beliefs about human interaction or motivation. But in her heart she had the forethought, wisdom to manage her home. This was acceptable to her family and aligned well with her strong faith.

Through her experiences and knowledge about parenting, Bonita's mother had common sense to provide a safe, secure, loving, disciplined and supportive home environment. Even in Bonita mother's absence, her children knew what was expected of them. She knew her children were not perfect, however, the home expectations were clear.

Bonita was fortunate to have a family who loved and cared for her. Both parents were present and active in her life. Today's families are more diverse and multi-layered. This story epitomize a faithful, strong, focused mother who made it clear to the world that her children and family came first.

(2) Pearl of Wisdom

Johari window

The second pearl of wisdom that manifested in the story, "Mama said..." is the Johari Window. This communication model of self-awareness was developed by two psychologists, Joseph Luft and Harry Ingrham. The model allows us to examine how to give and receive feedback when it involves two individuals. This model is useful because it helps to illustrate the relationship of Bonita and her mother.

Clearly, Bonita was on the receiving end of feedback from her mother. In a small way, her mother also benefit from the interaction. They learned from each other. However, Bonita had more to learn simply because she is a child. Let's take a look at the Table 3. You can see how the Johari Window manifested in their relationship. They become more self aware of their actions and its effects on others.

Below is an illustration that will help you to understand how the four panes are used. Keep in mind the idea is to show how two individuals can get to know and understand each other better. This concept was not used by Bonita and her mother. What is significant about this communication tool is its relevance.

Table 3 - The Johari's window

1 Known Self Things we know about ourselves and others know about us	2 Hidden Self Things we know about ourselves that others do not know
3 Blind Self Things others know about us that we do not know	4 Unknown Self Things neither we nor others know about us

It takes two or more individuals to communicate. That is why we call this 'interpersonal communication.' What does this look like? People communicate for different reasons. Most of these reasons are common to most people. Individuals share their interests, likes, dislikes, and reveal their emotions.

Johari's Window helps individuals understand what it is like to reveal information about each other. This awareness is made up of four panes that can be plotted on a grid showing the degree of what makes up the four "selves." Looking at the Johari Window, you see that the four panes are categorized as the open, blind, hidden and the unknown self.

As with Maslow, this model is appropriate for the story, Mama Said… because it aligns well with Bonita's experience and the relationship with her mother. This model is particularly interesting because the model frames the discussion about the importance of self-esteem, confidence and Bonita's awareness of who she is.

In the story, "Mama Said...", Bonita's mother spent much of her one on one time with Bonita to help her express herself. This task did not come easy for Bonita. Yet, if her mother had to assess where Bonita would fall on the Johari Window, she would probably place her between open and blind quadrants. When prompted, Bonita opened up to her mother.

When it came to school, the Johari Window pane changes. In the story you find that the fear of math encourages her to shut down resulting in missed assignments. Bonita was looking at her situation with narrow lens. Yet, her mother was able to get through to her. Bonita's mother was able to share her own personal stories to help Bonita open her mind to unseen possibilities.

This pearl of wisdom aligned with the Johari Window is an extremely useful and meaningful tool to help students realize their own potential in becoming confident communicators. This tool is also important for parents to practice in their homes. The benefits are many. It will allow parents to spend quality time with their children. It will allow children to feel like they matter because they have their mother's ear. It erases any misconceptions children may have about their own self worth.

This practice will take them a long way in developing stronger communication skills. The technique is most useful when communication has come to a halt.

It's important to keep in mind that this is a tool to facilitate discussion. A parent would need to facilitate the conversation with younger children at the elementary level. Middle and high school age children can work independently.

In the story, Bonita's mother talked directly to her. This is encouraged too. Using both methods can be extremely effective to opening the communication process. This survey is also available in a table format for shorter responses.

The next page provides a Student Self-regulating Survey to assist students in identifying and recognizing their need to self-express. It is a good tool for any student to use to assist them in moving from an "unexpressive" frame of mind to a "call to action" frame of mind.

Mama said...It's the small victories that count!

Self-regulating Survey For Students

- Who do I admire?

- What would I like to be when I become an adult?

- What do I care about?

- What do I already know about my interest?

- How will I let others know about my interest?

- Who would want to know about my interest?

- Given what I know now…How do I plan to become the best person I can be?

- What do I need to do to become the person I was meant to become?

- If I could be anywhere in the world, where would I be and why?

(3) Pearl of Wisdom

Block's Community: A Structure of Belonging

Community: A Structure of Belonging

The third model introduced in this book is based in scholar Peter Block on Community. The foundation of his theory rests on the idea of communities being a structure of belonging.

Block argues the importance of all stakeholders (i.e., educators, parents, business communities, social services) taking responsibility for creating a community that works for everyone. He argues that "collective change occurs when individuals and small diverse groups engage one another in the presence of many others doing the same." He points to entities such as schools, businesses, social agencies, churches and government that do not work well together.

Block paints a bleak picture of the current climate. Chances of collaboration is impeded because individuals may not feel as hopeful about their future as they once did. The current climate tends to be divisive instead of working towards a goal promoting common good. His position is on point because I personally observed the frustration from colleagues, parents, students and community advocates about the lack of urgency to solve problems together as a community.

Block is advocating for a movement that encourages collaboration that lead to healthy communities. He believes the key for effective community transformation is "…to structure a way of crossing boundaries where people become connected to those they are not used to being in the room with."

Block provided a new lens for looking at today's issues to start the dialog. It takes two people to communicate. An example of how Block's ideas are manifested in "Mama Said…" is reflected when Bonita's teacher welcomes a phone call from Bonita's mother. The phone conversation allows teacher and mother to make a connection. It is that experience that builds the relationship.

As Block argues, to get people together to start the real dialog has to be approach below the surface. He provides the notion of possibilities over problem solving.

Block recommends that we move away from our traditional way of thinking about community and problem solving. He identifies the current language below:

- Identify A Need
- Study and analyze a need
- Search for solutions
- Establish goals
- Bring others on board
- Implement
- Loop back

Block invites stakeholders to consider a very different view at advocating and building community towards action. Let's take a look at his notion of action.

"If we are to value building social fabric and belonging as much as budgets, timetables, and bricks and mortar, we need to consider action in a broader way."

Here are his examples:

- Would a meeting be worthwhile if we simply strengthen our relationship?
- Would a meeting be worthwhile if we learn something of value?
- Suppose in a meeting we simply stated our requests of each other and what we were willing to offer each other. Would that justify our time together?
- Or, in the gathering, what if we only discussed the gifts we wanted to bring to bear on the concern that brought us together. Would that be an outcome of value?

Block's ideas are a far cry from what we are used to. But maybe his ideas are not so far off. This process would require a complete paradigm shift in the way parents view educational issues specific to student learning and perhaps teaching. Equally important the educational community would need to embrace and adjust to new ways of building relationships and community.

Block is describing what he believes constitutes action in our communities. His approach seems inviting and welcoming. The big question that need addressing is: Would stakeholders be willing to lay down preexisting notions about what it takes to work together and solve real problems facing our families and educational communities? I think Block is on to something that provides value. What do we do together to move into action?

Can Block's approach create better opportunities for open communication?

Would parents like Bonita's mother be on board? Sure, and I'll explain why.

Bonita's mother was wise and understood a school community could be a place to seek out resources. The best resource available to Bonita and her mother was the teacher, Ms. Williams. This is where Block's argument finds a home with a parent such as Bonita's mother. Without physically gathering at the school to address Bonita's concern, her mother had total access to the school community. Block believe "It is not that we are gathering for the sake of gathering. Or gathering to get to know each other. We come together for an exchange of value and to experience how relatedness, gifts, learning, and generosity are valuable to community."

It is for this reason Block's ideas are relative in our school communities today.

Block's research stem over a period of time, made more relevant today. Having a structure of community is not a new concept. A sense of community was relevant decades ago. I think as a society, we have become robotic in the way we communicate with each other. In school communities, the pressures of meeting testing deadlines has moved pertinent issues such as teaching and learning in the back of the classroom, limiting opportunities to build community that works for everyone a bit tarnished.

Bonita's mother understood the value of community. She took the initiative to contact the teacher, Ms. Williams. In turn, Bonita's teacher saw the possibilities of engaging a parent. Eventually Ms. Williams extended the relationship by offering other services available to her daughter, Bonita.

If we really want to see positive change and welcome a new way to solve problems, it can be done. We have to be willing to embrace the ideas of others with open arms and mind.

Bonnie J. Edwards

DISCUSSION...
Self-reflective Models for Extended Teaching and Lifelong Learning

(Educators, Students, and Parents)

Bonita's Transformation
A Pearl of Wisdom

Mama Said...Be The Cool, Calm and Confident Communicator (CCCC) Model was born out of a need and desire to improve communication skills in families, among educators and to improve students' experiences. As educators, you get to see dynamics play out in all types of school and community settings. In my opinion, there were patterns of unhealthy interactions among staff, students, and families I observed in school settings that needed attention. Bonita, the character in the book, "Mama Said..." began the dialog for us.

Communication melt-downs in any social environment can test the patience of anyone. In many cases the immediate reaction creates an environment of confrontation resulting in negative relationships. research suggest that even children experience communication melt-downs. By implementing appropriate strategies as described in the following communication model, educators, parents, and students will improve on their ability to listen with clarity and build lasting relationships based on respect and compassion. The story, "Mama said…" illustrates this well in how mama applied her pearls of wisdom to help Bonita overcome her communication challenges.

Bonnie J. Edwards

Maslow Hierarchy of Needs
(more defined)
Bonita's Social Model

Psychological needs

Let's take a look at how Bonita's psychological needs were met. She lived in a loving and nurturing home. How do we know this? We know this by the close bond she shared with her mother. The moment Bonita walks into the front door after school, Bonita quickly and cheerfully seeks out mama, "Hi mama, I'm home." Her mother's voice sort of magically appears from the warm kitchen. It seems the two were awaiting this union. Imagine the moment, mother and child anticipating the moment to see each other. Bonita yearns to get a glimpse of her mother's smile, and her mother cheerfully responds, "How was your day at school Bonita?"

    Clearly, this tradition was set in mama's household for a long time. This was pretty much the routine most days of the week for Bonita. At home, Bonita's basic needs were established and met. She had the safety and security of knowing that her mother was home to receive her. This was possible because her mother was a business women working in a cosmetic industry that allowed her to modify her schedule to meet the daily needs of her family. Another example of how Bonita's psychological needs were met was the satisfaction of knowing that she would have a hot meal prepared upon arriving home from school. Her mother made sure the family had a nutritious meal prepared most days of the week. Some Sundays, Bonita's mother allowed Bonita to cook the big Sunday meals. Bonita succeeded in doing this well by learning how to cook from her mother. Her mother would often say, "A good cook also keeps a clean kitchen." Bonita knew that this was her mother's way of teaching her how to cook well and how to take pride in doing something nice that the family could enjoy.

Safety needs

Bonita shared a room with her sister and enjoyed the camaraderie with her sister is another example of how Bonita's security stayed intact. She had her siblings to interact with. Even in the sibling lineup, Bonita and her twin brother were in the middle of the sibling tree. They probably clanged more to their mother. Another example of Bonita's sense of safety and security is when her mother asked the eldest daughter to help Bonita with her math assignment. Her mother and father expected the children to get along even in disagreement. In some households, fathers were considered to be the disciplinarians. Most times both of Bonita's parents shared in this process.

Love and Belonging needs

In today's culture our view of family is different from generations past. There are many serious communication breakdowns among family members. Sometimes we allow our pride (I don't need anybody, No body understands me…) to get in the way of healthy communication. This can disrupt any opportunity to strengthen and build up family relationships. In the story, Bonita's mother wanted Bonita to know that she mattered. Bonita's mother illustrated this well in the story during this dialog after Bonita expressed frustration during and after her tutoring session with her sister, LeAnn, "Bonita, God never said life would be easy. We will have good and bad days." It is important to point out that much of Bonita's frustration hinged on her lack of confidence in herself to solve a math problem. Her mother was determined to help and encourage her daughter to do and be her best. She was able to accomplish this by sharing her own personal experiences and how she pursued resources to help herself.

Bonita's mother knew that in order to get her daughter to trust and believe in her abilities she would have to offer a pearl of wisdom using a parable, "I remember one day I was struggling and no one was home to help me when I needed it. Being the eldest child, my little brothers and sisters looked up to me all the time. Daddy was busy working on the farm and mama had the little ones to tend to. I had to rely a lot on myself. Times were so hard for us back in the day. We needed electricity not just for ironing but for light. Imagine doing your homework in the dark? But getting back to school, I knew school was a place I could get help with my assignments. So, I asked a lot of questions when I didn't understand something. You have to learn how to do that too Bonita."

Did Bonita's mother succeed in connecting with Bonita?

Bonita's mother illustrated the importance of believing in one self and speaking out. Bonita's mother would tell her daughter to never give up. Her mother knew that Bonita never felt comfortable when she perceived a challenge. The lesson her mother wanted to get across to Bonita when she encounter others at school or in the public is that it is OK to ask questions about anything you may not understand. This was a challenge for Bonita in school. In Junior and High school Bonita always felt challenged and believed she wasn't good enough. She loved herself but for reasons only known to Bonita, at a deeper level Bonita lacked self-confidence. At home, Bonita was comfortable, safe, secure and loved and most of all she loved being at home with her mother.

Her mother exemplifies what 'authoritative parenting' is and what it does. These types of parents set high expectations for their children. They are firm yet encouraging. Bonita's mother embraced the idea of "Be A Cool, Calm and Confident Communicator." This is what she believed. Bonita's mother admired her daughter's good listening skills. Bonita teeth glittered every time her mother complemented her on her communication skills. Unknown to Bonita, she didn't realize just how far that skill would help her and shaped her personality throughout her personal and professional life.

She understood Bonita's academic challenges and did what any responsible parent would do. Bonita's mother loved, supported, and encouraged her daughter. researchers (Steinberg, Lamborn, Dornbusch, Darling 1987,1988) argued that "Parents also influence children's achievement through their direct involvement with school activities, such as helping with homework or course selection or attending parent-teacher conferences, and through the specific encouragement of school success, both explicitly and implicitly, by setting and maintaining high performance standards."

Here is another illustration of how Bonita's mother bonded with her daughter. Bonita's mother began to share her personal story with her daughter about being assertive and asking questions. Mothers who are in tune to their children's needs can see how these characteristics and attributes aid in building self-esteem and character in children.

Prayer was also encouraged in the Gladney household.

"Mama said…" Once you get your education, you got it. No one can take it from you!" Bonita listened and agreed with her mother despite this shadow of doubt looming over Bonita, suggesting that she may still have doubt in herself to solve a problem.

Self-Esteem needs

Clearly, Bonita's mother is strong, confident, calm and compassionate. She understood the importance of making deep connections with her children. From a highly confident mother lion to her curious young cubs, mom knew at some point she needed to trust and believe that Bonita would learn how to grow into her own self with the proper guidance.

As Bonita became an older teenager she began to venture out more. With that came more responsibility. Her mother started to trust her more with the small things, such as wearing age-appropriate clothing.

Self-Actualization needs

I am always amazed at how little children are able to tap into their interests and natural gifts. This was not the case for Bonita. To her credit, she enjoyed socializing with her friends and has extraordinary communication skills. For a young person, the term 'communication' in itself was too broad for a young mind like Bonita's to comprehend. Bonita struggled with identifying and connecting with her natural gifts and talents. However, her mother did understand the importance of helping Bonita embrace her natural gifts which happen to be communication, the very skill she struggled with.

Mama said...It's the small victories that count!

Bonita's Self-reflective Model

A model for facilitating teaching & learning

Objective:

Teaching Students How To Be Cool, Calm Confident Communicator (CCCCs)

Outcome:

Helping Students Become More Confident In Themselves and Teach Them To Trust Their Natural Talents and Gifts

Mama said...It's the small victories that count!

Lesson and Goals:

Objective: Teach Students How To Stay Cool, 'Calm,' Confident Communicators (CCCCs)

Outcome: Helping Students Become More Confident Players In Trusting and Believing In Their Natural Talents and Gifts

Stage 1 - Desired Results from Students

- Improved communication skills (Better listeners, critical thinkers, collaborators, problem-solvers)
- Create opportunities for themselves to communicate better and with compassion in various settings; classroom, playground, project-based learning team/group work
- Held to a higher standard of respect, empathy, awareness and compassion
- Students will create an environment where they can act out their natural talents

Bonnie J. Edwards

Bonita's Personal Reflection Tool Kit

A model for facilitating teaching & learning

Table 1

Bonita Knew	Bonita Had Questions About	Bonita Learned
Mama cared	How to receive help with her math assignment	To seek out help and discovered her confidence
Mama loved her	Her life at home, school, church	Mama also had fears growing up
Lacked the skills to solve her math problems	Why she had more difficulties than her siblings	There will be good and bad days
She could count on her family for support	How to use all of her resources (teacher)	Trust and believe in herself

Mama said...It's the small victories that count!

Bonita's Personal Reflection and Tool Kit

"What I Know"
Personal Reflection (continued)

- Given what I know now…How do I plan to become the best person I can be?

- What do I need to think about to become the person I was meant to become?

- What do I need to do to become the person I was meant to become?

- If I could be anywhere in the world, where would I be, and why?

Bonnie J. Edwards

Bonita's 'Pearl of Wisdom' Transformation

Self-regulating and Self-expressing

It is important for families (teachers, support staff, parents, siblings, extended family, and friends) to be patient and allow their love ones to go at their own pace. It is not uncommon for young people to struggle with the maturation process. Some students automatically know what they want out of life while others have no clue. It's more common with the later group. There is no time limits assigned to this strategy. This is a great exercise for parents or adults to engage in with their children or students. Bonita provides some interesting input on her dreams and fears. Also, this template can help students understand why some things interest them and why other things do not. It's a gateway into what they are thinking and why. A blank template of this model is available in the Appendix 1 section of this book.

It is important to note that younger students (2nd-5th) grades, could answer a few questions from informed adults and young mentors to generate interest and start the dialog leading to excitement to become part of something big.

On the other hand, older students (6th-12th+) could handle answering all of the questions to generate excitement and engagement. Appendix 1illustrates how this strategy is available to any student at any age. Completing the Personal reflection Model is encouraged because it provides a guideline for meaningful discussion for children with their parents/guardians and educators. Most importantly, it gives the process a voice. For students who are still in developmental years, they will need support from the adults within their circle of family and school community.

Demonstrating Understanding and the Transfer of Learning

As a result of this process, Bonita becomes… (CCCCs)

- Cool collaborator
- Calm listener
- Confident critical thinker / problem-solver
- Communicator

With this knowledge and new skill(s), Bonita will be able to:

*Create opportunities for herself, family and peers to communicate with compassion in the following settings (but not limited to)

- classrooms
- campus grounds
- public settings
- project-based learning

It is important that students play an active role in facilitating their own learning about topics that interest them. They must know and learn how to ask questions like Bonita did.

Bonnie J. Edwards

"Making The Case For Joyce Epstein's Six Types of Family Involvement"

(Sample Practices For Parents and Guardians)

Type #1 - Parenting
Help all families establish home environments to support children as students:

- Appropriate home conditions that support learning a each grade level
- Parenting Workshops
- Videotapes on parenting and child rearing at each age and grade level
- Parent Education and related courses for parents (e.g., GED, family literacy)
- Family support programs (e.g., health, related services)
- Consider Home Visits at transition points to pre-school, elementary, middle, and high school
- Neighborhood Meetings

Point to Ponder: My understanding of Neighborhood meetings is to bridge the communication gaps between families and school requirements. Meetings in other public locations may allow individuals to feel free to express themselves in environments that are less intimidating.

Epstein continue to explain that the results or outcomes for students, parents and teachers are positive. Some examples of these outcomes for students include an awareness of family supervision; respect for parents. For parents, an outcome would be an awareness of own and others' challenges in parenting. For teachers, an example of an outcome would be having respect for families' strengths and efforts and (or) having an awareness of own skills to share information on child development.

Type #2 - Communicating
Design effective forms of school-to-home and home-to-school communications about school programs and children's progress:

- Conferences with every parent at least once a year, with follow-ups as needed
- Language translators to assist families as needed
- Weekly or monthly folders of student work sent home for review and comments
- Parent/student pickup of report card, with conferences on improving grades
- Regular schedule of useful notices, memos, phone calls, newsletters, and other communications
- Clear information on choosing schools or courses, programs, and activities within schools
- Clear information on all school policies, programs, reforms, and transitions

Point to Ponder: When I taught in the public school system, communication was a big issue. We did not have enough of it. Some local school communities were better at reaching out to parents, staff and students. Communication is necessary in all facets of life, especially in school communities.

As in Parenting, Epstein continues to explain that the results or outcomes for students, parents and teachers are positive. Some examples of these outcomes in Communication for students include their own progress and actions needed to maintain or improve grades. For parents, an outcome would be an responding effectively to students' problems as well as reaching out to teachers easing the communication process with school and teachers. For teachers, an example of an outcome would be having an appreciation for and use of parent network for communications.

Type #3 - Volunteering
Recruit and organize parent help and support:

- School and classroom volunteer program to help teachers, administrators, students, and other parents
- Parent room or family center for volunteer work, meetings, resources for families
- Annual postcard survey to identify all available talents, times, and locations of volunteers
- Class parent, telephone tree, or other structures to provide all families with needed information
- Parent patrols or other activities to aid safety and operation of school programs

Point to Ponder: I can't say enough about the value of volunteering at your child's school. This is a difficult task for many families and (or) parents because of other responsibilities (e.g., work and school demands, illness) demanding your attention. It is possible.

As in Communication, Epstein continues to explain that the results or outcomes for students, parents and teachers are positive in Volunteering. Some examples of these outcomes for students include developing new skills in communicating with adults. More importantly, students gain an awareness of many skills, talents, occupations, and contributions of parent and other volunteers. For parents, an outcome would be you gain self-confidence about ability to work in school and with children or to take steps to improve own education. For teachers, an example of an outcome would be having an awareness of parents' talents and interests in school and children.

Type #4 - Learning At Home
Provide information and ideas to families about how to help students at home with homework and other curriculum-related activities, decisions, and planning:
- Information for families on skills required for students in all subjects at each grade

- Information on homework policies and how to monitor and discuss schoolwork at home
- Information on how to assist students to improve skills on various class and school assessments
- Regular schedule of homework that requires students to discuss and interact with families on what they are learning in class
- Calendars with activities for parents and students at home
- Family math, science, and reading activities at school
- Summer learning packets or activities
- Family participation in setting student goals each year and in planning for college or work

Point to Ponder: One of my fondest memories of my childhood is the presence of my parents. I was old enough to understand they had to work in order to provide for the family but they were never too busy to support me and my siblings in school and at home. They were in tune to the needs of their children. In the story, Bonita was free to express herself to her mother when she was struggling in school with her math assignment. Her mother provided the resources Bonita needed by having her oldest child, LeAnn help Bonita at home with her math assignment. Bonita's mother also reached out to the school teacher requesting help for her daughter. The teacher gave the time and attention needed.

As in Volunteering, Epstein continues to explain that the results or outcomes for students, parents and teachers are possible for students Learning At Home. Some examples of these outcomes for students include an improved view of parents as more similar to teacher and of home as more similar to school and to recognize their own self-concept of ability as a learner. For parents, an outcome would be having an appreciation of teaching skills and an awareness of child as a leaner. For teachers, an example of an outcome would be a recognition of equal helpfulness of single-parent, dual-income, and less formally educated families in motivating and reinforcing student learning.

Bonnie J. Edwards

Type #5 - Decision Making
Include parents in school decisions, developing parent leaders and representatives:

- Active PTA/PTO or other parent organizations, advisory councils, or committees (e.g., curriculum, safety, personnel) for parent leadership and participation
- Independent advocacy groups to lobby and work for school reform and improvements
- District-level councils and committees for family and community involvement
- Information on school or local elections for school representatives
- Networks to link all families with parent representatives

Point to Ponder: The practices mentioned above are really important within and outside a school community. Unfortunately, many local schools lack these types of resources or if they do have them, the attention on important issues may be misplaced or not given the attention these practices deserve. Everyone in a school community are wearing many hats so it is a challenge to identify individuals to take the lead and make these resources available and acted upon in ways that would contribute and result in positive outcomes for all stakeholders. It is important to seek many individuals (e.g., parents, students, teachers, support staff, business leaders, volunteers) with special talents, skills and gifts to improve conditions in a school community.

    As in Learning At Home, Epstein continues to explain that the results or outcomes for students, parents and teachers are possible. Some examples of these outcomes in Decision Making for students include an awareness of representation of families in school decisions. For parents, an outcome would be shared experiences and connections with other families as well as awareness of parents' voices in school decisions. For teachers, an example of an outcome would be an awareness of parent perspectives as a factor in policy development and decisions.

Type #6 - Collaborating With Community
Identify and integrate resources and services from the community to strengthen school programs, family practices, and student learning and development:

- Information for students and families on community health, cultural, recreational, social support, and other programs or services
- Information on community activities that link to learning skills and talents, including summer programs for students.
- Service integration through partnerships involving school; civic, counseling, cultural, health, recreation, and other agencies and organizations; and businesses.
- Service to the community by students, families, and schools (e.g., recycling, art, music, drama, and other activities for seniors or others).
- Participation of alumni in school programs for students.

Point to Ponder: The sample activities mentioned above are attainable. One of the activity's that's illuminating for me as a teacher is when I taught students about the importance of service to the community. During the holidays, I remembered escorting a dozen elementary students to a senior citizen home two blocks away from the school. We walked to the home after a heavy snow fall the day before. Upon arriving, the children sang, "This Christmas" to the senior citizens with all their might in a small gathering room, perhaps a space designated as a lunch room. I still remember how beautiful the students sung and the expression of gratitude and joy on the faces of the residents. The students wanted to return to visit them on Valentine's Day.

As mentioned in Decision Making, Epstein continues to explain that the results or outcomes for students, parents and teachers are possible. With regards to Collaborating with Community, some examples of these outcomes for students include an awareness of careers and of options for future education and work as well as specific benefits linked to programs, services, resources, and opportunities that connect students with community. For parents, an awareness of school's role in the community and of community's contributions to the school. Adding, activity increases parents' knowledge and use of local resources by family and child to increase skills and talents or to obtain needed services. Outcomes for teachers would be an awareness of community resources to enrich curriculum and instruction as well as gaining knowledge, providing helpful referrals of children and families to needed services.

Mama said...It's the small victories that count!

For Parents of Middle and High School Students
"The Keeper of the Fire"

The Keeper of the Fire

Parents/Guardians,
What does it mean to be the Keeper of the Fire?

- Request to have a group discussion with other parents, teachers, administrators and support staff at your child's school.

- The school communities love to hear parents stories that helps to deepen understanding, make connections and build relationships.

The Keeper of the Fire

"My mother was the keeper of the fire in my life. Mama set the course for me because she was the flame I was seeking that kept me developing into an independent and responsible woman. Looking back, I can see her burning desire to help me become the best I could be. Today, her flame symbolizes the motivational light that keeps me inspired to keep going, learning, working hard, and inspiring others. Mama kept me on the straight path toward excellence. I am what I am today because my parents loved me and wanted me to succeed and have the best life."

~Bonnie J. Edwards

Mama said...It's the small victories that count!

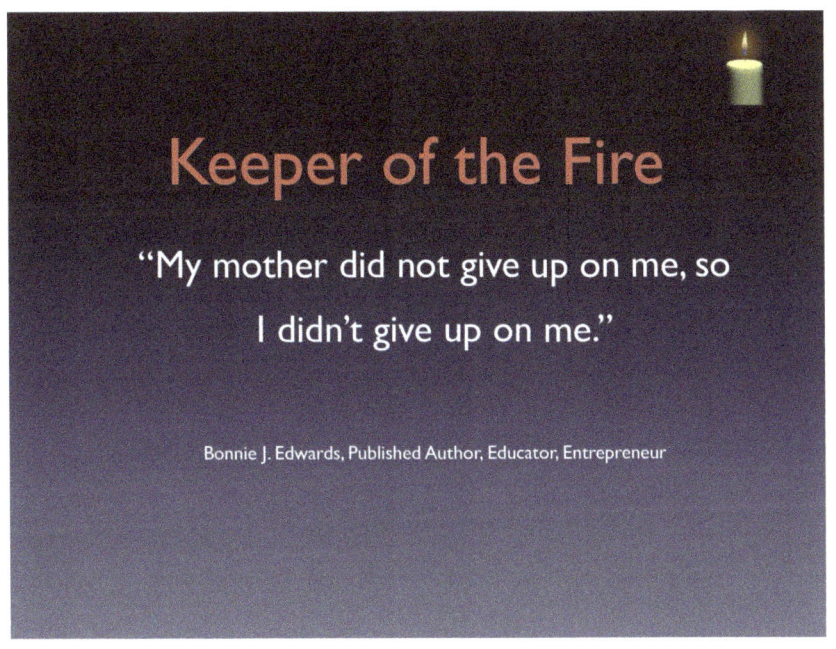

Keeper of the Fire

"My mother did not give up on me, so I didn't give up on me."

Bonnie J. Edwards, Published Author, Educator, Entrepreneur

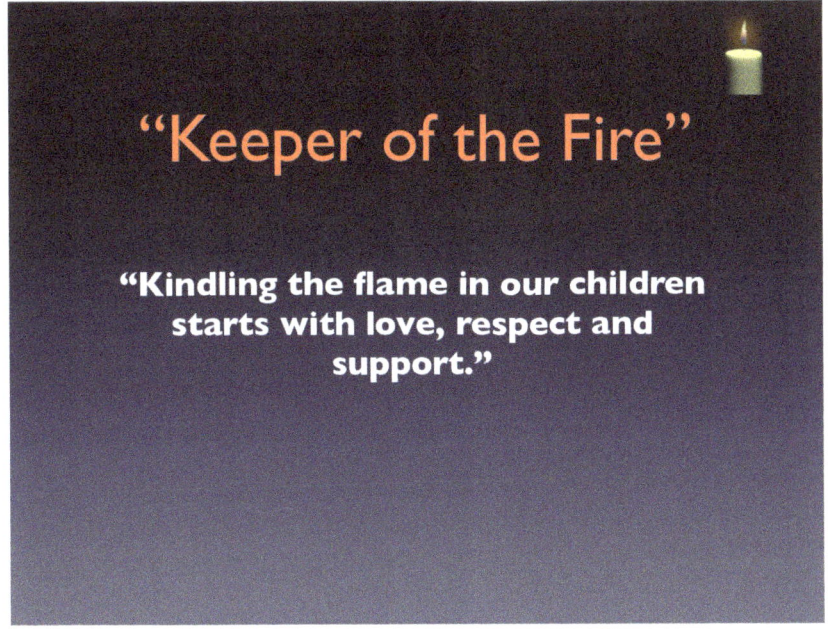

"Keeper of the Fire"

"Kindling the flame in our children starts with love, respect and support."

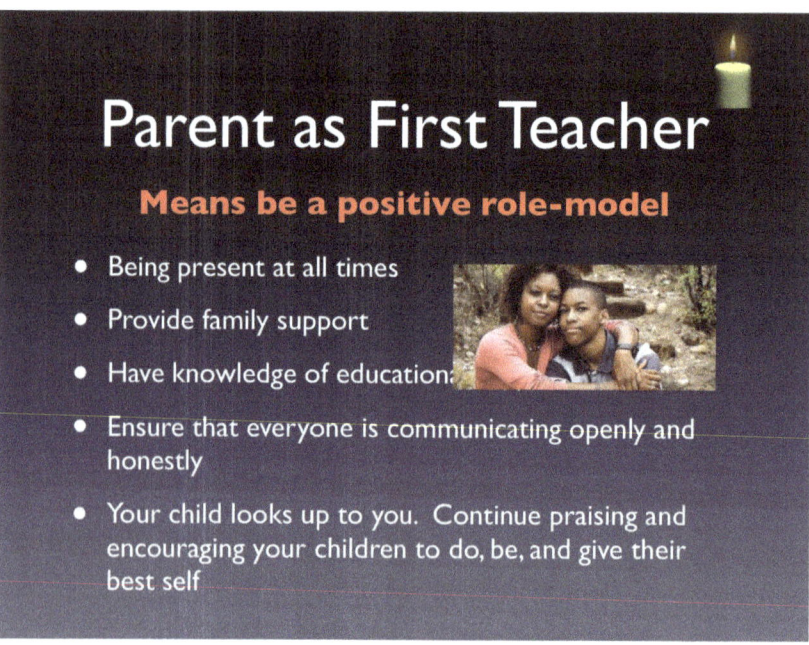

Mama said...It's the small victories that count!

Challenges and Barriers Parents Face

Characteristics:

- Lack of awareness of school processes/systems/navigating
- Limited time / busy schedules
- Illness/dependent children and aging parents
- Work demands
- School demands
- Lack of resources (e.g., funding, family and community supports and resources)

How do you become the Keeper of the Fire?

- We start with, "Know thy self," asking the right questions, getting the best answers and taking full advantage of the resources available to you and your sons and (or) daughters. Become self-aware.

Bonnie J. Edwards

Why is it important to know yourself?

- The better you are self-aware and informed...

The Better You Know Your Child

Here's how I know...

Mama said...It's the small victories that count!

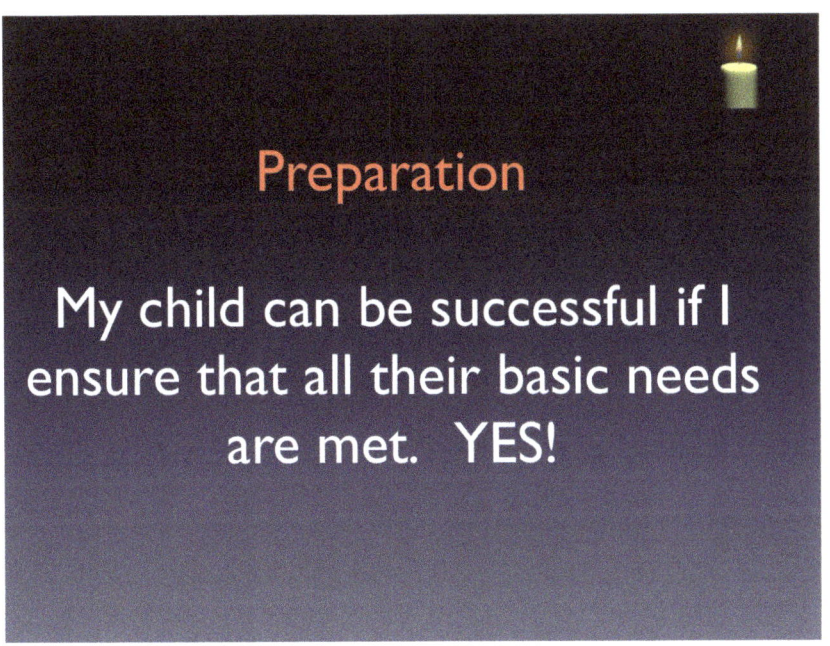

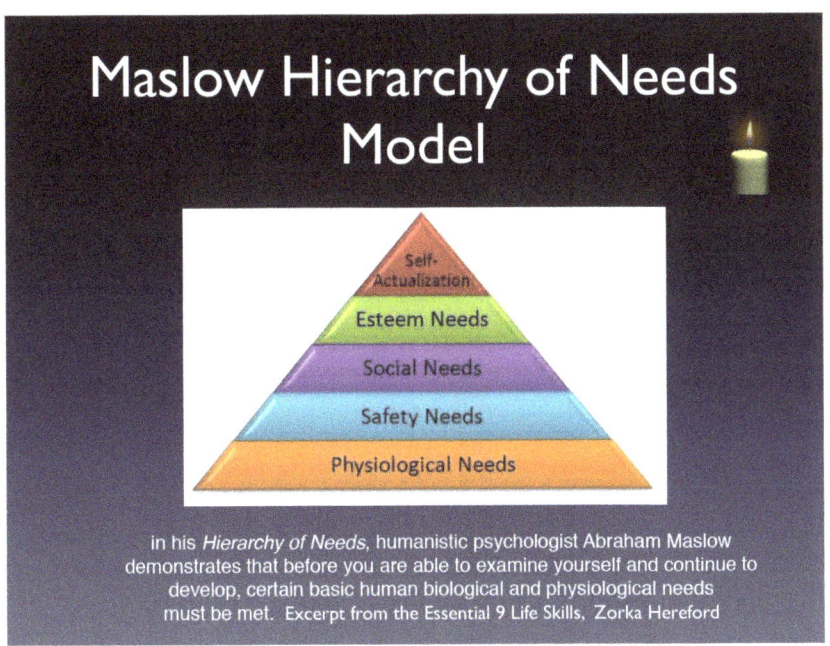

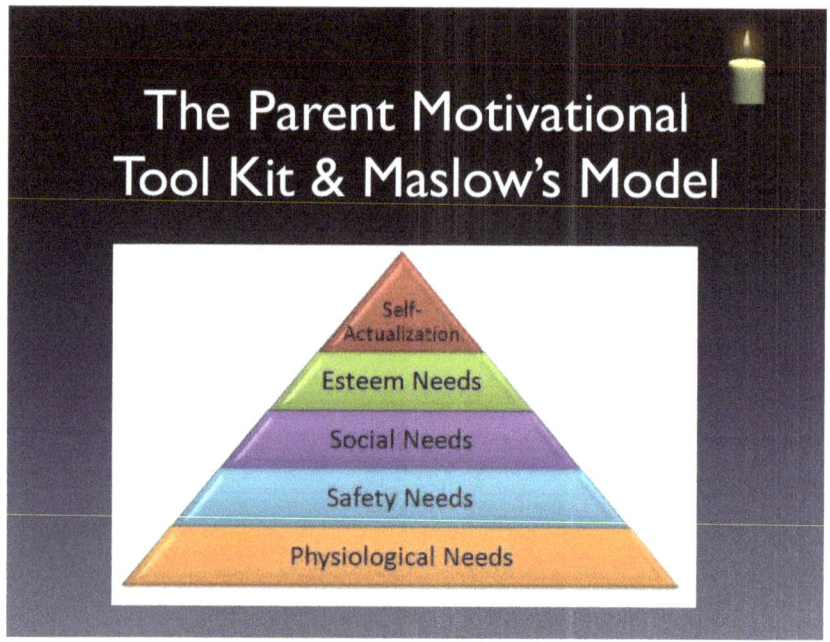

Meeting My Child's Safety and Security Needs

Preparation

- Secure, safe home, school and community
- Protection
- Free to self-express without judgment
- To have a calm and peaceful place to communicate study, and prepare
- Utilizing home, school and community resources

Ensuring A Sense of Belonging for My Child

Preparation
Step 3

- To know they are cared for
- Teach them to care for others
- To belong - They matter
- To get along with others
- To be protected and loved

Bonnie J. Edwards

Meeting My Child's Self-esteem Needs
Step 4
Preparation (Home)

- Do they feel confident?
- Have I helped them experience success?
- Have I encouraged them to strive for excellence?
- Have I taught them to accept responsibility & consequences for their decisions and behavior?
- Achievement
- Status or Station in Life

Meeting Self-actualization Needs
Preparation
Step 5

- Personal growth
- Fulfillment
- To soar like an eagle
- Fulfillment
- Born to succeed, to achieve, to be excellent

Epstein's Six Types of Family Involvement

- Research suggests that positive parent involvement equates to student achievement.

Epstein's 6 Types of Family Involvement that Works!

- Consider having a group discussion at your child's school.
- Align Epstein's Framework with your child's personal and career goals.

Preparing Your Child for College and University Admissions Requirements
What do they want?

Submit an application at the college/university website career fairs/ open house
Meet with a College Enrollment Advisor with your child
Provide your child's ACT/SAT Scores
Provide college/university with high school transcripts
Accept invitation to tour college/university campus
Help your child select a program of their interest
File for Financial Aid with help from campus office
Have a knowledgeable person (family, counselor) assist you through the process

What does my child need to be successful with ACT/SAT?

- Your child need to sit down with you first
- Your child need to discuss their dreams, goals, interests, aspirations, fears, hopes with you early in life, when they old enough to understand and express their thoughts
- Your child need to talk with the school's counselor to set goals, testing dates, interests, fears
- Your child need to take ACT/SAT serious & study hard
- Your child need you to believe in them

Consider Setting Expectations and Goals with Your Child Early in Life Together

ACT Prep
Setting Goals for Your Child

- Communicate openly and honestly
- Praise and encourage your child to do their best work
- Prepare your child to use all school and community resources available to them
- Allow them to take full responsibility for their own learning by writing down their personal goals

Where can I get help for my child for ACT/SAT Testing?

- Various local or online testing centers
- School & District resources are great
- Ask about the "Career and College Readiness" Programs
- Be prepared to pay a fee for testing or inquiry about a financial wavier

Generally speaking...Tips on Remedial / Bridge Programs offered by Colleges and Universities

Parents consider the following:
* Associate Program (2) year options: Community Colleges do not require testing for entry
*Inquire with the college Admissions Office w/concerns and Qs
*Students can take transferable Associated-level courses to help them with admissions requirements
*Programs that focus on transitioning to four-year colleges/ Universities
*Programs offering Time-management skills
*Programs focused on specific subject matter (e.g., Fine Arts, Math, Biology, Engineering, Education, Music Therapy)
*Programs that offer Associate Degree programs
*Consider Enrollment Challenges: GPA score below 2.0
*Consider Enrollment Challenge:s ACT score below 14

Khang Academy
Online Resources are available

- Online Tutors (Free!)
- Real time feedback
- Great resource for entire family
- App also available for downloading

https://www.khanacademy.org/college-careers-more/college-admissions/making-high-school-count/modal/v/overview-making-high-school-count

A Model of Transformation

Appendix 4

Admiration	Aspire To Become	The Effort
Who do I admire?	What would I like to be when I become an adult?	What do I already know about my interest?
	What do I care about?	Who would want to know about my interest?
	How will I let others know about my interest?	Who would want to know about my interest?

A model for making connections and building brighter relationships

Lesson and Goals

Educator as Facilitator of Learning
Cool, Calm, Confident Communicator
(CCCCs)

Objective: Instruct Educators on How To Be The Cool, Calm, Confident Communicator (CCCCs)

Outcome: Helping Educators Become Confident Advocates For Their Students and for Themselves Through Self reflection

Educator's Self-Reflective Model

How did Ms. Williams transform Bonita into a confident student using her pearl of wisdom as an educator?

Appendix 5

What I Know	What I Have Questions About	What I Learned

Bonnie J. Edwards

The Case For Character Education Could Lead to a More Caring and Compassionate Society

The Case For Character Education Integration into a K-12 School Curriculum

My Graduate Studies Program in the Department of Education at a local college I attended revealed to me the possibilities and implications for integrating Character Education Curriculum in K-12 schools. I became motivated to learn more about the issues at hand. I admit, I was intrigued by the possibilities of integrating Character Education in a school's curriculum. This mission became my "call to action" for my colleagues and anyone who was interested in creating a culture of caring, respectful, responsible, and a compassionate citizenship.

According to The Rebirth and Retooling of Character Education in America (2012), Sojourner, argued that, "The American founders recognized that "educating for character" was essential to the success of a democratic society because a healthy democracy demands civic virtues, such as voluntary compliance with laws, respect for the rights of others, concern for the common good and participation in public life." Years later, I've discovered that we have good reason to revisit the concept of integrating Character Education into our K-12 schools. It is important to note that there are mixed perspectives on the issue among scholars. It is also unclear as to what parents really want for their children from a public school mandate for educating their children. It appears that some parents value content and preparation for college admission. Other parents value the idea of knowing that their son/daughter have the capacity to be compassionate and respectful toward others. I wonder if our school systems can prepare students for both ideas?

Currently, many schools in urban communities utilizes the Positive Behavioral Intervention System, known as PBIS to address negative student behaviors. When I was a practicing educator in K-12 urban school environments, our school enrolled approximately 280 students attending in the 2013-14 school year. The PBIS program had proven to be successful in counteracting negative behaviors that would fall into several incident categories. This data was reported out on a monthly basis through summary detail from the urban school district's incident referrals; listing loitering, verbal abuse, personal/physical safety, and classroom disruption. A detailed account with graphs provided specific data analysis of the degree and frequency of the reported incidents.

Issue(s)

The area of most concern addressed in this report was the number of incidents and the frequency of the incidents in the classroom during instruction. A deeper analysis of understanding was needed to determine the cause of the classroom incidents. This narrative summary only provided a brief explanation of the problem.

The PBIS system is a way for schools and districts to counteract negative behaviors into positive outcomes. However, I believe the PBIS system only addressed the issues from an external award system. This approach does help with some students. In this framework, students were expected to follow the major social/behavioral themes of PBIS related to respect, responsibility, and safety for self and others. This is important. But, I do not believe it addressed the intrinsic nature of the developing adolescent intellectually, and socially. The school also provided a second type of behavioral intervention program called Second Step. This program addressed some of the internal or intrinsic needs of students. However, it is only a "microcosm" of the bigger problem with building characteristics in children such as empathy, respect, personal safety, integrity, and civic responsibility for all students.

In keeping with best practices for a viable character education program, I believed a solid and quality Character Education curriculum was crucial and necessary for the intellectual and social survival for all students. This program would also enrich peer to peer relationships within the school community and among all staff.

Most if not all people agreed that the school community is important. Students spend most of their waking hours in a school socializing with adults and their peers. It is vital for students to know how to communicate appropriately and when behaviors are socially acceptable and unacceptable in a school setting.

It is my opinion that the best place to teach these characteristics are in a classroom setting from a quality comprehensive Character Education curriculum. I believe the Eleven Principles of Character Education sponsored and implemented by the Character Education Partnership (CEP) program can be the key to a more engaging, caring, respectful and enriched staff and student body.

Solution

Research has shown and it is reasonable to expect that an educated citizen would have the capacity to show empathy toward others and work collaboratively with others in a system that would require collaboration among its citizens. How might we build a student's intellectual capacity that would allow them to show empathy toward others and work collaboratively in a system that benefits others? There is one system that may provide some answers. The National Character Education Partnership (NCEP) is a flagship program which has a long standing history and practice in defining the characteristics of Character Education. Locally, the Character Education Partnership CEP (1993), provides a Self-Assessment Tool for schools and districts as a guide to follow as they address whether character education quality standards are practiced in K-12 schools. CEP, a nonprofit, nonpartisan, and nonsectarian organization, "supports the beliefs that the ethical, social, and emotional development of young people is as important as their academic achievement."

What does the NCEP say about the principles of Character Education? The NCEP has identified eleven principles of character education that could apply to all schools. Here, I will identify what CEP says about empathy, compassion, and collaboration to reinforce the notion that this quality program is good and necessary for schools.

Principles of Character Education addressed in this narrative (Principles: #2, #3, #4, and #5)

Empathy

According to CEP, effective Character Education defines "character" comprehensively to include thinking, feeling, and behavior as identified in Principle #2. Once a school or district has established the foundational principles of what is valued as good character, the staff takes the necessary steps to ensure those core values such as developing empathy for others and having a sense of responsibility are acted upon through inspirational exemplars in literature, history, sports, the media, etc.,). CEP is on point. An example of how we embrace these core values like empathy is in how we spend our time during major holidays such as the Dr. Martin Luther King Jr., Day holiday. It is a day that many school districts recognizes and encourage their student body and staff to participate in community service activities such as volunteering in neighborhood clean-up, painting homes and helping at food pantries. It is when we embrace the core values that bring us together as a community that gives students and staff a sense of pride and belonging.

Compassion

Effective character education uses a comprehensive, intentional, and proactive approach to character development specific to all grade levels. One major component applicable here is in how well the classes are conducted. In Principle #3, classrooms routines address students' need for belonging, autonomy, and competence. Additionally, classrooms are respectful of students and engage them in ways that develop traits such as responsibility, fairness, and caring. A great example of this is when school administrators encourage field trips to visit senior citizen homes and read poetry to residents or entertaining them with other genres of literature. The residents may be home-bound and may just need to know that somebody cares.

Effective character education creates a caring school community. In Principle #4, the school makes it a high priority to foster caring attachments between adults and students. More specifically, students perceive staff as caring; the school makes provisions for students and teachers to meet in social settings to help them grow. One other major component addressed in this principle is that a school makes it a high priority to help students form caring attachments to each other. An example of this is when teachers and students create classroom environments in which respect and kindness are the standard (e.g., through class meetings). Teachers and students note caring acts and give compliments when they occur and correct unkind remarks when they occur. Last, the local school makes it a high priority to foster caring attachments among adults within the school community. For example, staff members make efforts to develop caring and respectful relationships among themselves. In a caring system, school staff would welcome parents and the broader community to participate in the democratic experience of students. Keeping in mind, the changes would require closing the existing gap that sort of separates key people (e.g., parents, teachers, community-at-large).

Collaboration

Effective character education provides students with opportunities for moral action. One of the major elements in Principle #5 is when the school sets clear expectations for students to engage in moral action in terms of civility, personal responsibility, good sportsmanship, helping others, and service to school and community. One other example would be the staff model; endorse, teach, and expect good sportsmanship, civility, compassion, and personal responsibility. Another component of character education applicable in democratic education is when schools provide students with repeated and varied opportunities for engaging in moral action in the larger community. Students are engaged in these opportunities and are positively affected by them. I agree with CEP, in that collaboration is extremely important if we want students to take personal responsibility as we participate more in a global world. In a democratic educational system, students would be expected to learn and work cohesively with their peers. by collaborating about what makes education works, who benefits from diverse perspectives, ensures well-rounded and caring learners.

The greatest "take away" for promoting character education characteristics in a school is creating the avenues for all students to benefit and succeed. The possibilities can be endless if appropriately implemented. A democratic education ensures that students will be literate, kind, compassionate, critical-thinkers and problem-solvers.

Cost factors

The cost reflects the needs and desires of the district and (or) local school communities.

Summary

Again, a solid and quality program such as the Eleven Principles of Character Education can be the catalyst for building a strong foundation for preparing students and staff for improved relationships and extending that relationship into a larger school community. When principles of character education are embedded and implemented in an educational system, we become witness to more giving of the heart, more literate student body, more on point in our academic and social perspectives. These principles embodies good character in students and the school community they represent. Parker (2011) states it well, "attend to the gifts and capacities of all others, and act to bring the gifts of those on the margin into the center." Considering the challenges educators, parents, and students face, we can not wait, it is time to try something different that may just work.

My Reflections and "Mama said...It's the small victories that count" Lessons To Live By

Bonnie J. Edwards

Memory Lane

To My Cherished reader,

This is an exciting and blessed time for me because I get to share with you some of my most special moments with my mother. As a young lady, I remember how challenging I was in my teens. But, my mother was relentless when it came to having my basic needs met. My mother saw my struggles and supported me throughout those informative years of my development. My mother also saw my natural talents and abilities and created opportunities for me to channel those gifts. My mother's pearls of wisdom continues to influence and sustain me today. She was stellar, yet gentle in her discipline. She was an honorable wife, devoted mother, grandmother, spiritual advisor and mentor. Best of all, our mother was in tune to us. We mattered to her. My mother never wavered in her love, patience and compassion for us. She had the heart to appreciate each of us as individuals. In her own way, she was able to make each of us feel worthy and loved. I am reminded of the song, "Your Grace and Mercy" by the Mississippi Mass Choir. Because my mother was of strong spiritual faith, through God, she was able to get me through the ups, downs, and turn arounds. I am my mother's daughter. My mother's legacy lives on in our hearts and my wish for you is that you hug your mother stronger and longer. As a gift to you, I want to share this special poem I keep close to my bedside that was written on Valentine's Day by my mother over fifth-teen years ago.

Mama said...It's the small victories that count!

"Mama said..."
"Trust and Believe"

"Mama said..."

"If you take time to relax you will find peace of mind."

Mama said...It's the small victories that count!

"Mama said..."

"The sky is the limit."
–Carolyn

Bonnie J. Edwards

"Mama said..."
"I Love You"

Mama said...It's the small victories that count!

"Mama said..."
"Have A Great Day!"
–Donald

"Mama said..."

"God will trust you with the big things when you show you can handle the small things."
–Carl

Mama said...It's the small victories that count!

"Mama said..."

"When things get tough pull yourself up by your boot straps and keep moving."
–Ronald

"My favorite quote from mama is what mama would say to me out of the blue, "I love you." Hearing those three words coming from mama made me feel wanted."
—Tommie

My Mama would give you the most gentle, warm, and loving "Hello" when you entered the room. Her smile would light up the whole house. Just her mere presence would make everything right in your universe.
–Linda

Bonnie J. Edwards

Special tribue to my mother…
"Mama said..."
"Be Nice"

Even under the most challenging situations, my mother would say to me, "Be nice." Her calming voice and soft spoken words (all two of them) would immediately settle my mind and allow me to put any situation in perspective. Just the words "Be nice" showed me how easy it is to love others and reach out to offer kindness. Ephesians 4:32 teaches us to, "…be ye kind one to another, tenderhearted, forgiving one another, even as God for Christ's sake hath forgiven you." My mother's words have stayed with me all of my life and I continue to live by those two small words.

Cary

(My Husband and Editor, "Mama Said…")

Appendix 1
Self-regulating Survey For Students

- Who do I admire?

- What would I like to be when I become an adult?

- What do I care about?

- What do I already know about my interest?

- How will I let others know about my interest?

- Who would want to know about my interest?

- Given what I know now…How do I plan to become the best person I can be?

- What do I need to do to become the person I was meant to become?

- If I could be anywhere in the world, where would I be and why?

Bonnie J. Edwards

CCCCs
Activity & Practice Model

It is important that students play an active role in facilitating their own learning about topics that interest them.

Appendix 2

Admiration	Aspire To Become	The Effort
Who do I admire? *I admire my mother, father, and my pastor. Mama said I can be anyone I want to be.*	What would I like to be when I become an adult? *I want to be like my mother, and maybe a nurse.*	What do I already know about my interest? *I know I like to help others. Having friends is important to me.*
	What do I care about? *I care about my being around other people. I like having fun and I'm curious about a lot things.*	Who would want to know about my interest? *My parents want to know.*
	How will I let others know about my interest? *I'm not sure but mama will know. I'll talk to mom.*	Who would want to know about my interest?

Mama said...It's the small victories that count!

Lesson and Goals

Parent/Guardian as Facilitators of Learning

(CCCCs)

Objective: Instruct Parents / Guardians on How To Be The Cool, Calm, Confident Communicator (CCCCs)

Outcome: Helping Parents/Guardians Become Confident Advocates For Their Children

Parent/Guardian Self-reflective Model

Appendix 3

What I Know	What I Have Questions About	What I Learned

References

Block, P. (2008, 2009). Community: The Structure of Belonging. Barette-Kohler Publishers. San Francisco, CA.

Edwards, B. J. (2011). Mama Said. Authorhouse Publishers. First Edition. Bloomington, IN.

Luft, J., and Ingham, H. (1955). Johari Window: Self-awareness model. retrieved from the Internet 05/26/2016.

Maslow, A. (1968) Maslow Hierarchy of Needs. retrieved from the Internet 05/26/2016.

Steinberg, L., Lamborn, S.D., Dornbusch, S.M., Darling, N. (1987, 1988) Impact of Parenting Practices on Adolescent Achievement: Authoritative Parenting, School Involvement, and Encouragement to Succeed. retrieved from the Internet 05/26/2016.

RESOURCES

Joyce L. Epstein, Ph.D., et. al., Partnership Center for the Social Organization of Schools: Sample Practices, 3505 North Charles Street Baltimore, MD 21218-3843
John Hopkins School of Education, School of Education Faculty Professor 2800 North Charles Street, Baltimore MD 21218
(414) 516-8807
Areas of Expertise:
Administration, Supervision and Leadership, Counseling and Human Development, Education in the Health Professions, Special Education and Gifted Education, Teaching and Learning
Epstein's Framework of Six Types of (parent) Involvement

The Haberman Educational Foundation National Center for Alternative Teacher Certification Information
Dr. Martin Haberman "Teacher Talk"
When Teachers Face Themselves: What Makes A Star Teacher?
4018 Martinshire Drive, Houston, Texas 77025-3918
Fax/Phone (713) 667-6185

Gloria Ladson-Billings
Kellner Family Chair in Urban Education, Department of Curriculum & Instruction, University of Wisconsin-Madison
464C Teacher Education Building
225 N. Mills Street, Madison, WI 53706-1707
Office: 608-263-1006
giladson@wisc.edu
2005-2006 President of the American Educational research Association
Author of the critically acclaimed book, *The Dreamkeepers: Successful teachers of African American Children*, *Crossing over to Canaan*

The Danielson Group LLC Charolette Danielson, Founder
The Framework for Teaching (Enhancing Professional Practice: a Framework for Teaching, 2007)
P.O. Box 7553, Princeton, New Jersey 08543
(609) 535 - 2053
https://www.danielsongroup.org/charlotte-danielson/
contact@danielsongroup.org
Mission: The Danielson Group seeks to advance the understanding and application of Charlotte Danielson's concepts in the educational community, connect them to other areas of knowledge, and enhance the professional practices of educators to positively impact student learning. Retrieved from https://www.danielsongroup.org/charlotte-danielson/.
June 15, 2016.

The Johari Window Graphic reaching Enduring Agreements
Retrieved from http://rea-agreements.com/blog/2010.03.01%20-%20March%202010%20-%20Self%20Awareness%20in%20Conflict.html.
June 15, 2016.

The Maslow Hierarchy of Needs Pyramid
Cognitive Sciences Stack Exchange
Retrieved from http://cogsci.stackexchange.com/questions/169/does- evidence-support-maslows-hierarchy-of-needs. June 15, 2016.

The Maslow Hierarchy of Needs Table 1
Rediscovering the Later Version of Maslow's Hierarchy of Needs: Self-Transcendence and Opportunities for Theory, research, and Unification Mark E. Koltko-rivera; New York University and Professional Services Group, Inc.; review of General Psychology Copyright 2006 by the American Psychological; Association 2006, Vol. 10, No. 4, 302–317
1089-2680/06/$12.00 DOI: 10.1037/1089-2680.10.4.302

Retrieved from http://academic.udayton.edu/JackBauer/readings%20 595/Koltko rivera%2006%20trans%20self-act%20copy.pdf. June 16, 2016.

The National Academics of Sciences - Engineering - Medicine Board On Science Education, Division of Behavioral and Social Sciences and Education
The National Academies
500 5th Street, NW, Washington, DC 20001
Tel: 202-334-2164, Fax: 202-334-2210, e-mail: bose@nas.edu

"**Road To Deeper Learning In Common Core Mathematics Standards**"
"The new Common Core standards emphasize deeper learning of mathematics, learning with understanding, and the development of usable, transferable mathematics competencies. The standards identify several important learning goals: critical thinking, problem solving, constructing and evaluating evidence-based arguments, systems thinking, and complex communication."

"Unlike competencies in the cognitive domain, those in the intra-personal and interpersonal domains are not particularly prominent in the standards. However, the standards for mathematical practice give some attention to the intra-personal competencies of self-regulation, persistence, and the development of an identity as someone who can do mathematics." Retrieved from http://sites.nationalacademies.org/cs/groups/dbassesite/ documents/webpage/dbasse_084153.pdf June 9, 2016.

CONTACT US

To make requests for speaking and (or) professional development
Please contact:
B.J. Edwards Professional Development & Training
Author, Educator, Speaker, Entrepreneur
P.O. Box 18764 Milwaukee, Wisconsin 53218
(414) 943-2510
Email: bjedwards@wi.rr.com
Website: www.mamasaidwhattome.com

Follow Us On...
Facebook
Twitter
Instagram
LinkedIn
To purchase 3rd Edition
Mama Said…by Bonnie J. Edwards, contact the online booksellers and other retail stores:
Start with:
Barnes and Noble.com
Amazon.com

"Mama said..."

"Trust in the Lord with all thine heart, and lean not unto thine own understanding. In all thy ways acknowledge Him, and He shall direct thy paths."
Proverbs 3:5-6

Daddy   Mama

Mama said...It's the small victories that count!

The author/publisher, educator, and entrepreneur, Bonnie J. Edwards is featured in a family portrait with her siblings, Linda, Carl, Carolyn, Tommie, (twin) Bonnie, Donald (twin) Ronald.

Mother, Dorthel and father, George are featured above. Bonnie is married to Cary, both live in Milwaukee, Wisconsin. Their children are Danny, Lisa and Mildred.

"Dream"

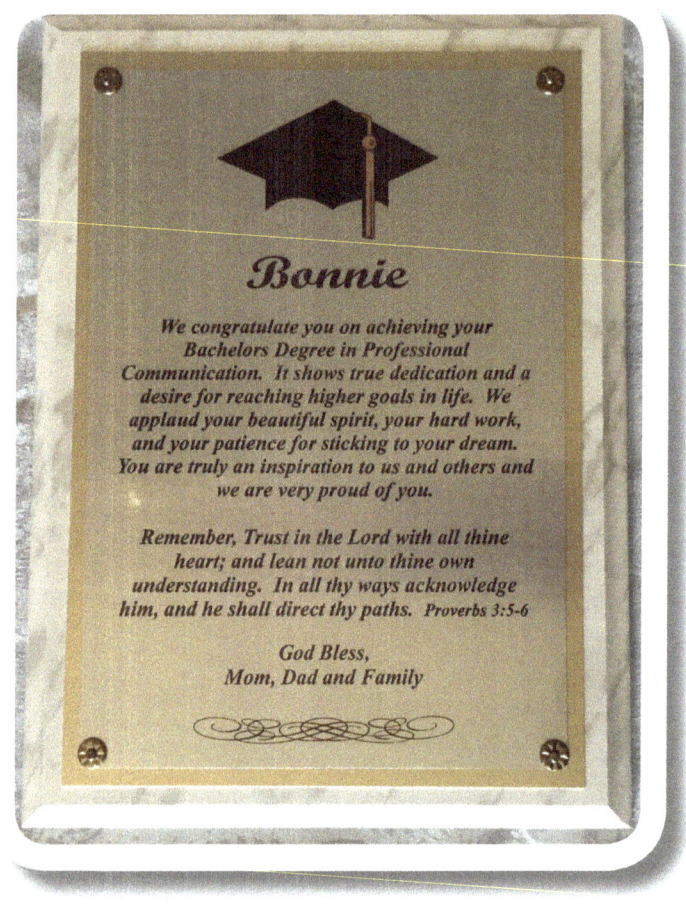

My mother would say, "Think twice before you speak because everything that comes up ought not come out." Her words still radiates within me to this day, as she sings, "All I have belongs to God."

Herbert McCoy
Waukegan, Illinois

My mother would say, "Bennie, if you do good, good will follow you."

Rev. Dr. B.J. Gaston
Milwaukee, Wisconsin

Growing up my mom always said, "that's what you get for being responsible." I didn't understand what that meant until I became an adult. To me, it means people may not react the way you thought or you may not receive what you expected for being responsible and doing the right thing, but, the ultimate reward really *is* being responsible and knowing you did the right thing.

Adrienne l. Carr
New York, New York

I attended a reading of this book. The characters were so vivid that I could see them as author Bonnie J. Edwards read. The lighthearted humor was infectious to all who listened and could relate to individual characters. The picture painted at the reading made me rush home to purchase this book to share with my family.

Mildred L. Starks
Milwaukee, Wisconsin

Mom would always tell us, "If you give something to someone, always give them your best."

Carrie Anderson
Denver, Colorado

This is a wonderful story. It speaks to the basic needs of every child. All children need someone to be there for them like mama is for Bonita when she needs her. Bonita is very fortunate in that she also has a great family; parents, brothers, and sisters that provide support in her hour of need. Beyond that there is her teacher who encourages Bonita, gives her some direct instruction, and then directs her towards yet another source of help.

Parents and educators should also make use of the communication section included in the back of the book. Communication is the best tool we can use to learn ways in which someone is in need. Often a child such as Bonita is struggling and no one listens or ignores the pleas for help. In Bonita's case her mama saw and heard, then followed through with constructive and loving advice. Communication is a two way street which means that an environment of safety and trust needs to be provided for a back and forth exchange to take place.

The communication section provides the tools needed to better understand that basic needs must be met before a child is receptive to learning. Many children need to have a caring mama or educator to help them but they also need to be able to communicate what their needs are and it is here that the communication section provides the means to help with that aspect.

Use this book to help children understand that it is okay to ask for help. Also, use information within the book to assist in ways to build a communication bridge within a family or classroom.

Dr. Janis Giblin
Milwaukee, Wisconsin

Milton Keynes UK
Ingram Content Group UK Ltd.
UKHW021236100324
439113UK00005B/114/J